Stevenage

Pioneering new town centre

Historic England

You are now entering the

NEW TOWN
of
STEVENAGE

Stevenage

Pioneering new town centre

Emily Cole, with Elain Harwood and Edward James

 Historic England

Front cover
Stevenage Town Square and Queensway in 2021.
[DP278964, Patricia Payne]

Inside front cover
Stevenage town centre viewed from the north in 2018.
[33749/026, Damian Grady]

Frontispiece
Signboard for Stevenage new town, Baldock Road, in a photograph of 1952.
[Stevenage Museum]

Inside back cover
Schematic map of Stevenage on the south side of the Town Square clock tower. It was produced by Carter's of Poole and apparently designed by Leonard Vincent.
[DP233328, Derek Kendall]

Back cover
Joy Ride by Franta Belsky, unveiled in Stevenage Town Square in September 1958.
[DP233347, Derek Kendall]

Published by Liverpool University Press on behalf of
Historic England, The Engine House, Fire Fly Avenue, Swindon SN2 2EH
www.HistoricEngland.org.uk

Historic England is a government service championing England's heritage and giving expert, constructive advice.

The views expressed in this book are those of the authors and not necessarily those of Historic England.

Images (except as otherwise shown) © Historic England Archive

Figs 45 and 81: [© and database right Crown Copyright and Landmark Information Group Ltd (All rights reserved 2021). Licence numbers 000394 and TP0024.]

First published 2021

ISBN 978-1-80085-599-1

British Library Cataloguing in Publication data
A CIP catalogue record for this book is available from the British Library.

For more information about images from the Archive, contact Archives Services Team, Historic England, The Engine House, Fire Fly Avenue, Swindon SN2 2EH; telephone (01793) 414600.

Typeset in Georgia Pro Light 9.25/13pt

Page layout by Carnegie Book Production
Printed in the Czech Republic via Akcent Media Limited.

Contents

Acknowledgements

The research, fieldwork and writing for this book, and the Historic England Research Report on which it is based, were undertaken by Emily Cole with Elain Harwood, Senior Architectural Investigators at Historic England.[1] Emily Cole also carried out the picture research, while the final chapter on the future of Stevenage town centre was written by Edward James, Historic Places Adviser in Historic England's East of England region. The material draws upon Elain Harwood's ongoing work into new towns nationally, which is due to be published by Historic England and Liverpool University Press in the near future, but also relies upon a great deal of new primary research. It should be noted that the progress of work – especially the historical and picture research – was affected by the COVID-19 pandemic and the closures of libraries and archive centres nationally, including the Historic England Archive.

In undertaking the historical research for this book, particular use has been made of the Stevenage Development Corporation papers held by Hertfordshire Archives and Local Studies, the Development Corporation's successive journals *Quarterly Bulletin* and *Purpose* (1951–66; held by Stevenage Museum) and local newspapers held by the British Library. New photography has been undertaken by James O. Davies, Derek Kendall and Patricia Payne, and graphics have been supplied by John Vallender.

For their help in providing information and images for this book, particular thanks are due to Jo Ward and Alan Ford of Stevenage Museum; Tom Pike, Lucy King, Christina Barnes and Zayd Al-Jawad of Stevenage Borough Council; and the staff of Hertfordshire Archives and Local Studies, including Chris Bennett. I am also especially grateful to Martin Friend and David Rixson of Vincent & Gorbing Ltd, John Vincent, and my colleagues at Historic England, including Natalie Gates, Edward James, Tony Calladine, John Cattell, Katie Carmichael, Joanna Smith, Matthew Bristow, Wayne Cocroft, Gary Griffin, Nicky Cryer and Esther Blaine.

Others to have kindly provided information, images and consent for reproduction are Eva Bryant and Nigel Wilkins of the Historic England Archive, Kathryn Morrison, Simon Bradley, Julia Skinner of Francis Frith, Stacen Goldman of the Framingham History Center, Anthony Wilkinson of the RIBA, Vanessa Winstone of the National Brewery Centre, Kenneth Thomas of Heineken UK and Robyn Orr of Liverpool University's Special Collections and Archives.

It has been a pleasure working with Barbara Follett, who wrote the foreword for the book, and the team at Liverpool University Press and Carnegie Book Production. Special thanks are due to Alison Welsby, Patrick Brereton, Siân Jenkins and Sarah Warren.

Foreword

This is a timely book. Its publication coincides with the 75th anniversary of the founding of Stevenage new town and the start of a major programme to regenerate its once revolutionary town centre. Historic England, by telling the story of the development of Britain's first, post-war, new town centre in such a readable fashion, adds to our understanding of its historic significance as well as providing a useful reminder, as the centre's ageing infrastructure is restored, of what it once symbolised.

That was hope. In 1945, the people of Britain, after another long and bloody war, were ready for radical change. Three-quarters of a century later, at the tail end of a terrible pandemic, the public mood is similar. Now, as then, we want to leave the deprivation, the disease and the insecurity of the past behind and build a kinder, greener and more sustainable future. Ebenezer Howard's garden city movement provided the post-war Attlee government with a model for this change and in 1946, after much consultation, the New Towns Act was finally passed. This piece of legislation, coupled with the Town and Country Planning Act of 1947, allowed the construction of 28 new towns in Britain over the next 50 years. Stevenage was the first.

Stevenage was also the only one of the 28 to build a town centre which uncompromisingly reflected the ideals of the new towns movement. In this impressively detailed book, Historic England focuses on this centre, not the town. The descriptions of its buildings – which included a theatre, a ballroom, a leisure centre, a cinema, a clinic, a swimming pool and a bowling alley – as well as its covered walkways, cycleways, open spaces and free parking, are illustrated by numerous photographs and drawings. These give the reader an understanding of why, from the 1950s until well into the 1970s, Stevenage new town centre was so famous. They also highlight the achievements of Stevenage Development Corporation, the body appointed to oversee the design and construction of the whole town. Their task, which was based on the new towns movement's firm belief that architecture and design should promote happiness and a sense of community as well as utility, was not an easy one. But, in the words of the then Minister of Town and Country Planning, Lewis Silkin MP, they were 'building for a new way of life'.

New ways of life are rarely without opposition and the inhabitants of the original town of Stevenage were vociferous and inventive in their disapproval. But Silkin was determined and the Old Town, as it is now known, became one of the new town's neighbourhoods. Its medieval shops and Georgian coaching inns remain, and, despite changes, it still retains much of its charm.

This is mainly because Stevenage new town centre was built on or around the old town centre. Its developers, keen to make a fresh start and avoid compromise, erected it on vacant ground to the south-east of the original centre. Most of the other new town centres of the period did not make this fresh start and, consequently, lack the coherence and unity which makes the Stevenage centre unique.

Almost 50 years later, as a keen parliamentary candidate, I took my first walk around Stevenage town centre. The Development Corporation was long gone, and despite the valiant efforts of its successor organisation, Stevenage Borough Council, it was a stained concrete shadow of its former self. Ever diminishing public funds, fragmented ownership and changing retail habits had taken their toll on its buildings and walkways. The art and the open spaces were still there but the landscaping was scrubby and many of the paving stones were cracked. The shops and cafés looked almost as tired as the premises they occupied and the water feature around the clock tower needed a good clean. It was obvious to me then that something, on a large and expensive scale, needed to be done to restore it. In 1997, as the newly elected Member of Parliament for Stevenage, I started the first Parliamentary New Towns Group to lobby for the funds to repair and renew these once proud symbols of a better way of life. Nine years later, as the Minister for the East of England, I would, again and again, see the damage that years of underfunding and neglect could wreak on flat roofs, wooden window frames and communal staircases in the other new towns of the region. Progress was made but it was piecemeal and infuriatingly slow. Today, almost 25 years since I first set foot in Stevenage, I welcome the start of the regeneration programme and pay tribute to the determined efforts of Stevenage Borough Council and others who have finally made it happen. There are, as there always are, differences of opinion over some aspects of the restoration, just as there were with the plans for the original new town. But, with patience and goodwill, I believe we can resolve these and give people back some of the pride they used to have in their town centre.

The people of Stevenage are the product of the practical idealism of the new towns movement, which enabled their parents and grandparents to leave the overcrowded, bombed-out suburbs of London and start a new life in the green fields of Hertfordshire. The earliest residents were mainly construction workers who laid the foundations of the new town and its neighbourhoods. They brought with them their skills and, as survivors of the Blitz, a sturdy resilience which, when combined with their trade's ability to organise, allowed them to play a vital role in the community organisations which sprang into being with the new town.

Thankfully, these community organisations have endured, mainly because the cooperative spirit that fostered their creation remains strong today. This is probably the greatest achievement of the visionaries who founded Stevenage new town. They did, as Silkin hoped, build a new way of life. One which, mainly thanks to the town's situation, layout, architecture and facilities, gave its inhabitants the time and space to connect with the people, causes and leisure activities that mattered to them. In other words, Stevenage Development Corporation managed to deliver the very qualities which made its brief so difficult – happiness and a community spirit, the very qualities that I found so attractive in 1995 and still do today.

Sadly, the Development Corporation did not do so well on the durability, or what this book calls 'the level of survival', of the infrastructure of Stevenage new town and its centre. This has affected the happiness and community spirit of its residents, and I fear that these qualities may not survive further decline. Fortunately, Stevenage Borough Council, whose motto 'The heart of a town lies in its people' reflects its priorities, is doing everything it can to prevent this from happening with its ambitious regeneration programme. I wish them well in this endeavour and look forward to the next stage in the development of this extraordinary town.

Barbara Follett, Member of Parliament for Stevenage 1997–2010
12 May 2021

Detail of relief sculptures of 1973 by William Mitchell, Scenes from Everyday Life, *within pedestrian underpass beneath St George's Way.*
[Patricia Payne, DP278125]

1
Introduction

Stevenage in north Hertfordshire is Britain's first post-war new town, its draft designation of 1 August 1946 confirmed on 11 November the same year. Like other new towns in the South East, it was sponsored and financed by the government and was built with the aim of providing overspill accommodation for Londoners. In 1954 it was claimed that 'Dissatisfaction with their housing conditions is the main reason why people wish to leave London for a new home in Stevenage'.[2] The aim was that the town would be self-sufficient and would offer residents ample employment, modern housing and a good range of educational and social facilities.

The new town of Stevenage included – around the town centre – an industrial area on the west of the railway line and a series of residential 'neighbourhoods' to the north, east and south. Each of these had its own hub of shops, community facilities and recreation spaces, while running through the centre was a valley left as open farmland. The old town of Stevenage was preserved as one of these neighbourhoods, to the north, rather than becoming the basis of the new settlement, as at the new towns of Crawley, Hemel Hempstead and Bracknell.

Design and construction of the new town was entrusted to Stevenage Development Corporation, a public body appointed by the government. It began work in 1946–7, following a Master Plan prepared by a team of planners from the Ministry of Town and Country Planning led by Gordon Stephenson. The Corporation's own architects and planners revised the town centre scheme into the early 1950s, with the final design approved in December 1954.

Construction of the town centre began in 1955, in an area comprising a roughly rectangular plot of land bounded by Six Hills Way (to the south), St George's Way and the Town Centre Gardens (east), Northgate and later Fairlands Way (north) and London Road/the Great North Road and later Lytton Way (west). Work started with the road network, bus station, car parks and shopping precinct, and then extended to offices, community, entertainment and public buildings.

The 'well-planned, well-built and thoroughly up-to-date' shopping centre was officially opened by Her Majesty The Queen on 20 April 1959, and was described as 'one of the boldest planning projects of its time' and an achievement 'not only for modern planning but also for local opinion', which was fundamental to the adoption of the pedestrian plan (Fig. 1).[3] Such was its success

Cross canopy at the east end of Market Place, built 1956–8.
[DP233298, Derek Kendall]

Figure 1
The former Co-operative store in the Town Square,
opened in June 1958, with its tiled mural by Gyula Bajó.
[DP233265, Derek Kendall]

that an extension of the shopping area was carried out in the early 1960s, with further extensions undertaken in the years up to the dissolution of Stevenage Development Corporation in 1980.

A civic centre in the north part of the town centre was an important component of the original scheme. However, new work at Stevenage was halted in 1961–2, due to government cuts and pending consideration of a proposal to increase the town's population from 80,000 to 150,000. In the end, this suggestion came to nothing, but the hiatus had serious implications for the town's development. The work of Stevenage Development Corporation inevitably lost some of its momentum, and although the civic centre was still being planned in the mid-1970s, it was abandoned shortly afterwards.

Stevenage is notable for its fully pedestrianised town centre – in 1956, it was described as 'the first pedestrian centre of its size in Europe'.[4] It was based upon an outline scheme of 1950 devised by the new town's Chief Architect,

Clifford Holliday, with the planner Gordon Stephenson and the American designer Clarence S. Stein, a pioneer in pedestrian planning between the wars. The separation of pedestrians from cars, experimental in Britain in the early to mid-1950s, soon became widespread: in 1959, it was stated by one writer that 'The traffic-free shopping street is clearly the norm for the future'.[5] Stevenage town centre is also striking for its levels of uniformity and integrity. Unlike other modern high streets, its buildings of the 1950s and 1960s were designed as part of a single concept under the same architectural team and survive well, with only a handful of major demolitions to date.

Now in its 75th-anniversary year, Stevenage is at a crossroads in its history. A major, £1 billion regeneration programme for the town centre is already underway, with more extensive and radical changes planned in the near future. Some of these even affect the first phase of the shopping precinct at its core, which was designated a conservation area in 1988, with the boundary amended following recommendations in 2010. The area currently contains two grade II-listed structures – the clock tower in the Town Square, which features a plaque commemorating the Queen's opening of the precinct in 1959, and the sculpture *Joy Ride* on the adjacent platform, unveiled in 1958. On the east side of the town centre, the Church of St Andrew and St George is also listed grade II.

Alongside consideration of the future of this experimental and significant town centre development, it seems fitting to celebrate its past. This book is intended as a tribute to all that was accomplished at Stevenage new town centre. In spite of the many challenges that beset the town from its earliest years and the limited funding available, the result proved worthy of all the efforts expended and the belief and dedication of locals and officials. Still, today, Stevenage boasts the most notable among Britain's post-war new town centres, and the development has had an important impact both nationally and internationally.

STEVENAGE

2 The new towns programme

The early years of Stevenage new town

Britain's new towns were one of the most remarkable achievements of the post-war years, a programme of far-reaching vision and ambition. Established by the New Towns Act of 1946, the programme built upon over 50 years of thinking and experimentation. It saw itself as the successor to the garden city movement begun by Ebenezer Howard, the founder of Letchworth Garden City in 1903 and of Welwyn Garden City in 1919. The movement was continued by Frederic Osborn and C. B. Purdom, who produced two important books following the First World War: *New Towns after the War* (1918, republished in 1942) and *The Building of Satellite Towns* (1925).

Howard conceived the garden city as a solution to the twin problems of urban congestion and rural decline. By 1940 the counties around London were becoming overrun by suburban development, while the capital remained overcrowded, its slum housing cheek by jowl with noxious industries. The Second World War provided an opportunity to assess the problems and plan for the future. In the County of London Plan of 1943, the town planner Patrick Abercrombie and John Henry Forshaw, architect to the London County Council, envisaged over a million people moving out of the capital. Abercrombie went further in his Greater London Plan of the following year (published in 1945), which proposed a ring of eight or ten new towns around London, including Stevenage and Harlow among the suggested locations (Fig. 2).

The concept of a new towns programme was taken up with enthusiasm by the Ministry of Town and Country Planning (formed in 1943) and by its minister from 1945, Lewis Silkin (1889–1972). Silkin had grown up in the East End and had been a member of the London County Council, which in the 1930s had introduced the first green belt legislation to control the capital's sprawl. He appointed a New Towns Committee in September 1945 to consider the organisation and management of the programme. The zeal of the committee's Chairman, Lord Reith, saw three reports and an Act of Parliament within a year. This has been described as 'the instrument of one of the greatest social experiments the world has known'.[6]

Stevenage's Master Plan in its 1955 form, as depicted in a tiled mural within Daneshill House (completed 1961). The town centre is shown in grey and yellow, next to the railway line.
[DP232449, Patricia Payne]

New town designation

Stevenage was Britain's first new town: a draft Designation Order was served on a site of some 6,100 acres on 6 August 1946 – five days after the New Towns Act passed into law – and this was confirmed that November. Seven more designations followed around London – Crawley, Hemel Hempstead and Harlow in 1947, Welwyn Garden City and Hatfield in 1948, and Basildon and Bracknell in 1949. Three towns in the Midlands and northern England were also designated – [Newton] Aycliffe (in 1947), Peterlee (1948) and Corby (1950) – along with two in Scotland (East Kilbride in 1947 and Glenrothes in 1948) and one in Wales (Cwmbran, 1949) (Fig. 3). All of these new towns sought to create socially balanced communities and to establish good living and working conditions by blending the best of town and country, including excellent facilities for shopping and entertainment.

At the proposed sites, the government's draft designation was followed by consultation and a public inquiry. The planning and construction of the new towns was entrusted to development corporations, unelected public bodies modelled on Reith's beloved BBC. The 1946 Act gave them the power to compulsorily purchase land and to grant or refuse planning permission for development within their designated area, with responsibilities for planning housing, industry, roads and a town centre akin to those of a local authority. Other functions such as schools, libraries, health centres and open spaces remained with the county and district councils. The development corporations reported directly to the Ministry of Town and Country Planning and its successors – the Ministry of Local Government and Planning (1950–1), the Ministry of Housing and Local Government (1951–70) and the Department of the Environment (1970–80). They were established for all 32 new towns designated across the United Kingdom between 1946 and 1970, with Hatfield and Welwyn Garden City sharing a single corporation.

Notably, Stevenage new town was established alongside an older settlement. This small market town can claim origin from Roman times through the presence of a rare group of burial mounds south of the new town centre, the Six Hills of AD 100, and the road running north from Verulamium/St Albans opened it to development. Edward the Confessor granted the estate in 1062 to Westminster Abbey and by 1281, when a weekly market was licenced, Stevenage

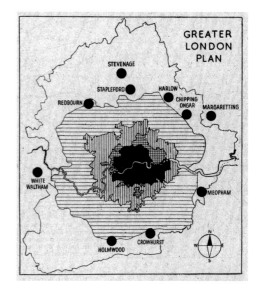

Figure 2
The ring of new towns proposed by Patrick Abercrombie's Greater London Plan of 1944 (published 1945).
[RIBA Collections]

Figure 3
Map showing the 'first wave' of British new towns,
designated between 1946 and 1950.

had become the area's largest settlement. Development moved away from its early nucleus around the parish church of St Nicholas to line the broad high street with shops and inns, and Stevenage became a prosperous coaching town (Fig. 4). By 1939 the town had a population of about 6,000 people, and this

Figure 4
The High Street of Old Stevenage in a
photograph of 1952.
[© The Francis Frith Collection]

number rose to almost 10,000 during the war when many businesses relocated from London. Stevenage Urban District Council had proposed its own modest development in the 1930s, and agreed in principle to the government's proposals for expansion in January 1945.

The site of the new town had much to commend it. It was adjacent to the mainline railway and the Great North Road or London Road (A1), there were adequate water supplies for the first housing, natural drainage was good and there was an existing administrative nucleus, as well as scope for a completely new town centre. However, the first months of 1946 saw hostility rise among the area's population – the writer E. M. Forster, a former resident of Stevenage, was among those who spoke out against development of the district, which he described as 'the loveliest in England'.[7] When Lewis Silkin addressed a public meeting on 6 May he made some tactless comments; there were shouts of 'Dictator' and 'Gestapo', the tyres of the ministerial car were let down and sand poured into the petrol tank.

Opposition, resentment and debate continued to dog the early history of Stevenage new town. A public inquiry on the draft Designation Order was held in October 1946, but the Ministry issued its final Designation Order on 11 November, and on 5 December it established the Stevenage Development

Corporation to plan a town for 60,000 people. The residents argued that Silkin had not conducted the public inquiry with an open mind, and took their case to the House of Lords. It was only in July 1947 that the Designation Order for Stevenage received final approval, and planning began in earnest at the end of that month.

Architects and planners of Stevenage new town

Figure 5
Gordon Stephenson at his desk at the Ministry of Town and Country Planning, November 1947.
[By courtesy of The University of Liverpool Library, D307/6/12/1]

Meanwhile, consideration turned to the layout of the new town at Stevenage. The initial work was begun in 1945, primarily by Gordon Stephenson (1908–97) and Peter Shepheard (1913–2002) of the Ministry of Town and Country Planning (Fig. 5). Both were former students of Patrick Abercrombie and had worked on the Greater London Plan. Later, Stephenson wrote of Shepheard, 'He was the architect-planner. I was the ideas man and hard-to-please critic'.[8]

Stephenson and Shepheard both hoped to be formally appointed to Stevenage Development Corporation, but in the end the position of Chief Architect and Planner went to Clifford Holliday (1898–1960), a planner typical of an older generation, though he too had worked with Abercrombie. A later Stevenage administrator described him as 'a gentle leisurely man the despair of his more pushing juniors'.[9] Shepheard was recruited as Deputy Architect, though he resigned after only nine months, failing to agree with Holliday about the plans for Stevenage. Stephenson turned instead to higher education, being appointed Lever Professor of Civic Design at the University of Liverpool in January 1948, though he went on to serve Stevenage Development Corporation as an occasional consultant.

In these early years, there was a fairly rapid turnover of chief architects at Stevenage Development Corporation. In 1952 Holliday left for the University of Manchester and was replaced by Donald Patterson Reay (1914–2002), who came to Stevenage from an identical post at East Kilbride new town in Scotland. Reay did much to promote the pedestrian town centre at Stevenage, but left in 1954 to take up a professorship at the University of California, USA.

It was at this point that the architectural team at Stevenage Development Corporation became more firmly established. The role of Chief Architect and Planner was awarded to Leonard Grange Vincent (1916–2007), who had joined the Corporation as Assistant Chief Architect in 1949 and was promoted as Reay's deputy in 1950. Vincent was Chief Architect until 1962, and continued to oversee work at Stevenage in the capacity of a consultant until the Corporation's dissolution in 1980 (*see* p. 35).

The layout of Stevenage new town

The earliest work on a Master Plan for Stevenage was undertaken in 1945–6 by Gordon Stephenson and Peter Shepheard along with others including the engineer Eric Claxton (1909–93) and the planner Tom Coote. This document aimed to set out the overall layout of the new town and to provide information on areas such as population, public services, the road system, cycle-way system and topography. An initial draft plan was completed in 1946, and used natural features and existing physical barriers such as railway lines to guide the proposed arrangement. The document was then revised by Clifford Holliday, the new Chief Engineer George Hardy and their staff. A finished version was submitted to the Minister of Town and Country Planning in August 1949, though in a public inquiry that October Holliday admitted that he had made few changes to Stephenson's scheme (Fig. 6).[10]

Like other new towns, Stevenage was based on the principle of neighbourhood planning, a concept which developed in both Britain and America during the inter-war years and which was fundamental to Abercrombie's County of London Plan of 1943. Stevenage's Master Plan envisaged a new town centre – located a mile south-east of Stevenage old town – bounded by six neighbourhoods. Old Stevenage was the first of these, plus five entirely new areas on the east, south-east and north-east of the new town: Bedwell, Shephall, Broadwater, Chells and Pin Green. Each of these areas was planned to house around 10,000 people and each had its own neighbourhood centre with facilities including shops, schools, churches and pubs.

There was a strong emphasis from the first on open space and landscaping. A consultant, H. Frank Clark, was succeeded by two young landscape architects employed by the Development Corporation, Gordon Patterson (1928–2020) and Gordon Howe. The draft plan of 1946 aimed for 13 acres of open space per 1,000 people, in addition to recreation grounds and school playing fields.

Figure 6
Photograph of 1949 showing the Corporation's planner Ron Pistorius comparing a relief model of the new town's site with the draft Master Plan.
[TopFoto]

A town-centre park was sited so that it could capitalise on existing natural features, while Fairlands Valley to the north-east was preserved from development, as were established small woodlands.

Holliday's most significant alteration to the plan for Stevenage was to these landscaping proposals. He produced a more detailed scheme for town gardens at Bedwell Plash near the new town centre, and linked the Fairlands Valley to the countryside beyond the town. Holliday hoped that 'It will be possible to pass on foot from one part of the town to another scarcely using a road at all by means of gardens, commons, parks and the Fairlands Valley'.[11]

The Master Plan for Stevenage was approved in February 1950, which meant that detailed design work and construction could begin. The document guided development of the new town until a revised plan was produced by Leonard Vincent in 1955.

Construction of the new town

The residents' legal challenge held up the start of building at Stevenage disastrously, and the slow production of the Master Plan further delayed progress. However, following its approval in February 1950 work moved forwards, focusing in particular on the construction of housing and the road network. The first dwellings in the new town were completed in 1951 in Broadview off Sish Lane, close enough to the old town to be linked to the existing drains. The first London family, Mr and Mrs Sulzbach with their young daughter, moved into 4 Broadview in March (Fig. 7).

Work then moved to Bedwell, which was the first of the new neighbourhoods to be developed, in 1952–3. Broadwater followed from 1953 and Shephall was begun in 1953–5. All the early housing was for rent, and was mainly formed of short terraces, similar to the cheaper housing at Letchworth, Welwyn and in many urban areas across England (Fig. 8). By 1953 Stevenage new town already had a population of 13,000, and by the end of 1954 – shortly after national building restrictions were lifted – the Development Corporation had built just over 3,000 houses. This represented significant progress, though Stevenage lagged behind Crawley, Hemel Hempstead and Harlow new towns due to poor management and the need for a comprehensive new drainage

Figure 7
Bob and Thelma Sulzbach with their son Robert outside
their home, 4 Broadview, Stevenage, in a photo of
c. 1961, taken ten years after they moved in.
[Stevenage Museum]

system. The neighbourhood of Chells was built from 1958 and Pin Green from 1962, to a heavily revised plan that doubled its population.

The new towns were expected to provide their own employment rather than add to London's problems of commuting, and incomers had to have a job in the town before they were offered a house. The establishment of an industrial area was therefore an early priority, and this was created in 1951 to the west of the main railway line – not far from the site of the town centre. The first factory in the new town was occupied by the Bay Tree Press in 1952, when the Corporation was first allowed to build standard factory units speculatively rather than for a specific lessee. Larger employers built their own factories, including de Havilland Propellers Ltd in 1953 (part of Hawker Siddeley from the early 1960s), Kodak Ltd in 1954 and English Electric Aviation Ltd in 1955. The latter became Stevenage's largest employer, merging with Vickers in 1960 to form the British Aircraft Corporation and in 1977, on nationalisation, British Aerospace.

Figure 8
Bedwell Crescent, part of Stevenage's earliest new neighbourhood, constructed in 1952–3.
[DP247675, Patricia Payne]

3

Plans for a pedestrian town centre

The most notable and pioneering aspect of Stevenage new town centre is its pedestrian shopping precinct. This traffic-free approach to planning was first suggested for Stevenage in 1946, when Peter Shepheard drew up outline plans in liaison with Gordon Stephenson. Both were then working for the Ministry of Town and Country Planning; appointments to Stevenage Development Corporation were only made from autumn 1947 (*see* p. 9).

Although a written description of the pedestrian scheme formed part of the Master Plan produced in 1946 and revised three years later, detailed design work was delayed initially. This was partly due to differences of opinion between the planners and existing residents about the exact location of the town centre. Hertfordshire County Council and Stevenage Urban District Council both argued that the area should be further east than proposed in the 1946 plan, in order to be more geometrically central to the new town as a whole. In contrast, Stevenage Development Corporation continued to support Stephenson's proposed location, not least because of the convenience of being adjacent to the Great North Road, the railway line and Old Stevenage. This matter was decided when in February 1950 the Minister of Local Government and Planning approved the Corporation's revised Master Plan, and design work on the town centre began that year.

However, there were further delays as the different options for the town centre were explored and as the controversial proposals for a pedestrian precinct were discussed. As a result, the design process for Stevenage town centre was comparatively long and drawn out, with an outline scheme only agreed in mid-1954 and detailed work undertaken in the following years. Ultimately, the designs produced under Leonard Vincent were probably improved by this delay – for instance, in being able to draw upon new constructional developments in curtain walling. On the other hand, this delayed process meant that Stevenage was not underway before comparable schemes such as Coventry's Upper Precinct and Harlow Market Square.

The rise of motor traffic

Until the early 1950s, the concept of pedestrian planning was generally unknown in Britain. Vehicle-free developments were few and far between,

Model of Stevenage town centre produced in c. 1959, viewed from the south-west.
[Stevenage Museum]

Figure 9
London's High Holborn in 1900, showing the huge
number of carts and other traffic which used the
thoroughfare.
[CC97/01653]

mostly limited to the shopping arcades and galleria which reached a height of popularity in the late 1800s and early 1900s. There were a handful of other pedestrian thoroughfares, some lined with colonnades for walkers. These included The Pantiles in Tunbridge Wells, Kent (begun *c.* 1698), Bath Street in Bath (built 1791–4) and Sicilian Avenue in Holborn, London (1906–10). Nevertheless, these were isolated developments with no wider influence on mainstream town planning. The vast majority of British high streets and shopping areas had shops set along what were often busy roads, thronging with carts, coaches, horses, omnibuses and other traffic (Fig. 9).

With the rise of motor vehicles from the early 20th century – and in particular from the inter-war years – such shopping areas took on a new character. Road traffic became increasingly dominant, and the potential dangers to pedestrians, tradespeople and indeed drivers accelerated rapidly. Between 1910 and 1928 the number of vehicles on the roads in Britain – including cars, buses, lorries and motorcycles – increased from 140,000 to two million. It had reached three million by 1938, four million by 1949 and well over five million by 1956.[12] In order to accommodate this multitude of new vehicles, the government embarked on a huge programme of road building, expansion and improvement.

As a consequence of this great change, road accidents increased – by 1956, 5,000 people were killed and over 200,000 injured each year.[13] Understandably, so did criticism of traditional shopping areas and calls for a more formal segregation of pedestrians and vehicles. For the civil engineer and planner Colin Buchanan, writing in 1956, 'The babel and whirl of traffic take all the pleasure out of using the town, and its considerable architectural character counts for nothing'.[14] The town planner Wilfred Burns was another who aired his views in this area, stating in 1959 that older shopping centres had during the inter-war period 'lost their interest as meeting places' and become 'death traps'.[15]

Particularly vocal about this subject was the traffic planner Herbert Alker Tripp of the Metropolitan Police, who wrote *Town Planning and Road Traffic* in 1942. Alker Tripp commented that

> Great streams of high speed traffic have suddenly invaded age-old towns and villages, in the streets of which people on foot continue to pursue their lawful occasions – just as they have for generations past. If that local populace cannot be completely withdrawn from the main streams of fast traffic which have invaded its haunts … then the main streams of motor traffic must be withdrawn from the local populace.[16]

Alker Tripp advocated shopping precincts for pedestrian safety, with vertical separation ('double-decker' schemes) seen as ideal. His ideas were later incorporated in the Ministry of Transport's manual *Design and Layout of Roads in Built-Up Areas* (1946), which for around 20 years served as the design guide for British traffic engineers.

Early pedestrian schemes

America

The difficulties and dangers of driving and parking motor vehicles in town centres were felt earlier in the United States than in Europe, due to higher levels of motor traffic. They were already being experienced by the 1920s, and led directly to the construction of shopping precincts – generally on the edge of towns or in new suburban developments. A pioneer in this area was the architect and planner Clarence S. Stein (1882–1975), whose work included the pedestrian shopping centre at the new town of Maplewood, Louisiana (1943).

The pedestrianised approach grew in popularity during these years, resulting in suburban developments such as the McLoughlin Heights shopping centre in Vancouver, Washington (1942), and the Linda Vista shopping centre in San Diego, California (1943). Of particular note is Shoppers' World in Framingham near Boston, Massachusetts (1951), designed by Morris Ketchum, Jr. In this pedestrian scheme, surrounded by car parking, a department store at each end ensured a good footfall through the site and helped to anchor the design (Fig. 10). A notable feature of these new precincts was their architectural uniformity, which was in sharp contrast to the diverse character of earlier, unplanned historic centres.

Figure 10
Shoppers' World in Framingham near Boston, a notable American pedestrian shopping precinct opened in 1951. [Framingham History Center]

Europe

In Europe as in Britain, some historic areas have long had separate pedestrianised arcades and walks, often within colonnades. However, in terms of wider pedestrian planning due to the rise of the motor car, the first steps were taken in the 1920s with the closure of some historic streets to traffic. The Kalverstraat in Amsterdam, a 16th-century shopping street, was closed to vehicles in stages from around 1924, earning it the title of Europe's 'first pedestrian shopping mall'.[17] Another early example of this type is Limbecker Straße in Essen, Germany, pedestrianised in 1927.

For larger-scale developments, the bar was set by the Lijnbaan, a new shopping street in the heart of Rotterdam in the Netherlands. It was commissioned in 1951 as a response to pre-war congestion and the bombing of the old high street nearby. Comprising 65 shops in six blocks, it was begun in July 1952 and completed in autumn 1953 to designs by Johannes 'Jo' van den Broek and Jacob Bakema (Fig. 11).[18] Europe's first purpose-built pedestrian street, the Lijnbaan proved highly influential, not least on Stevenage. It was

Figure 11
Bird's-eye view of the Lijnbaan in Rotterdam,
Netherlands, built in 1952–3.
[National Archives of the Netherlands]

Figure 12
The pedestrian shopping centre of Vällingby, Stockholm, Sweden, built in 1952–4.
[John Reps Papers, #15-2-1101. Rare and Manuscript Collections, Cornell University Library]

formed of blocks of two main storeys, joined by single-storey cross canopies providing shelter for shoppers. Originally, the scale of the development, reserved for high-class shopping, was comparatively modest; it was extended in 1966. In recognition of its status, the first phase of the Lijnbaan was designated a national heritage site in 2010, and it has been restored in recent years by Mei Architects & Planners.

Another influential European development was the central area of Vällingby near Stockholm, one of the Swedish settlements built on the 'Arbet-Bostad-Centrum' ('work-dwelling-centre') or 'ABC' model. This was an initiative of 1952 by the admired architect and Stockholm city planner Sven Markelius, who aimed to bring the variety and animation of city life to a series of new satellite towns on the edge of the capital after a 1930s development at Årsta was deemed too suburban. The earliest was Vällingby, with a central area of shops, offices and entertainment buildings constructed in 1952–4 (Fig. 12).[19] It is therefore exactly contemporary with the Lijnbaan. Vällingby's central zone was carefully restored as part of a regeneration programme in 2001–8, retaining the development's 'mid-century modern' character. For some years Stevenage and Vällingby enjoyed close links, and the influence of Swedish design can be clearly seen in Stevenage's town centre.

Beyond these developments, very few pedestrian schemes were completed in Europe in the 1950s – and none which formed an entirely new town centre. This reflects the fact that in the post-war period only Sweden boasted a programme of new settlements comparable with the ring of new towns established around London in the late 1940s and early 1950s. Other countries developed a new towns programme only much later – for instance, the group of towns established around Paris followed legislation in 1965, with large-scale construction beginning around 1970.

Great Britain

In Britain, H. Alker Tripp's work was taken up by Patrick Abercrombie and other planners, becoming increasingly influential, and by the end of the 1940s there was awareness of pedestrian schemes undertaken overseas, including the Kalverstraat. Even though most retail traders were adamant that the public preferred to shop in areas 'where there is a large volume of traffic with a resultant atmosphere of stir and bustle', the government (or at least the Ministry of Transport) felt this to be a statement 'of conditions as they exist rather than an indication of what the public would choose were other types of shopping areas available to them'.[20]

The first opportunity to put the new ideas into practice came with the rebuilding of cities after wartime bombing. In Coventry, the City Architect Donald Gibson introduced a pedestrian open-air shopping street into his plans for rebuilding. This was conceived after night raids in November 1940 had blocked Smithford Street; Gibson noticed that traffic moved more freely round Broadgate as a consequence, and produced initial designs for a new scheme in 1941. Four years later, the Coventry Corporation agreed to shopkeepers' demands to retain a cross road for vehicles, but over the pedestrian shopping street at right angles it remained firm and designs – with shops on two levels – were approved in 1947.

The first element of the innovative Coventry scheme was named the Upper Precinct, with buildings by Gibson and H. S. Hattrell & Partners. The detailed designs were produced in 1951–3 in a somewhat old-fashioned classically influenced style, and construction took place in 1954–6. The development was small and confined, with two ranges of shops joined by raised pedestrian walkways (Fig. 13). The second part of the scheme, the Lower Precinct, was built

Figure 13
Coventry's Upper Precinct, designed in detail
in 1951–3 and constructed in 1954–6.
[AA98/06068]

later – after Stevenage shopping precinct had been initiated. It was constructed in 1957–60 to designs by Douglas Beaton of the City Architect's Department in a more modern, Festival of Britain-influenced form than that used at the Upper Precinct, with two levels of shops around a courtyard containing the circular Lady Godiva café (Fig. 14). Meanwhile, the approach to the cross street was changed thanks to Gibson's successor, Arthur Ling, with Market Way completed as a pedestrian route in *c.* 1957.

Other British architects and planners conceived schemes related to that initiated at Coventry during the 1940s. Indeed, the interplay of thinking between various figures – many connected to Patrick Abercrombie – is complex, and it is difficult to unravel which are 'first' among the proposals and developments. In some cases, designs were produced early on, but these were not realised until several years later – as with Stevenage town centre. A pioneer was an unexecuted proposal for a pedestrian town centre at Ongar in Essex, one of Abercrombie's proposed new towns, drawn up by Peter Shepheard for the Greater London Plan in 1944 (Fig. 15). Through Shepheard, this has a direct link with the work later undertaken at Stevenage, though Ongar itself proved too expensive to develop. It was followed by Princesshay in Exeter, a narrow

Figure 14
The Lower Precinct, Coventry, built in 1957–60. It was altered shortly after this photograph was taken in 2000. [AA003483, James O. Davies]

Figure 15
Peter Shepheard's proposal for a neighbourhood centre at Greensted, Ongar, taken from Patrick Abercrombie's Greater London Plan (published 1945). [Courtesy of Paul Shepheard]

pedestrian precinct planned by Thomas Sharp in 1946 and begun in 1949 as part
of the city's reconstruction after war damage, though only completed in 1962.
Closer to Stevenage in form were the pedestrian shopping centre built in 1950–1
to designs by the architect-planner Frederick Gibberd at the LCC's Lansbury
Estate in Poplar, East London – part of the 'Live Architecture' exhibit of the
Festival of Britain – and the Broadwalk in Crawley new town centre, which
comprised parallel shopping arcades containing 25 shops, begun in late 1952
and opened in December 1954 (Fig. 16).

While designing Lansbury, Gibberd was also working at the new town of
Harlow, Essex, for which he produced a Master Plan in 1948, revised in 1952.
The Poplar precinct served as a model for a large neighbourhood centre built at
The Stow, Mark Hall South, in 1951–4 and also Harlow town centre, planned as
a series of pedestrian squares from 1947 and designed in detail in 1952–4. In
both cases, the Harlow Development Corporation intervened to change the
nature of the scheme. The Stow featured a road as completed, while the
Corporation's Chairman, Richard Costain, demanded that an access road should
also cross the central Market Place – the first part of the town centre scheme to
be built, in 1955–6 (Fig. 17). This meant that the original central area was not
wholly pedestrianised and though the access road was closed as early as 1964, its
outline can still be determined.

Figure 16
*The pedestrian shopping precinct of the LCC's Lansbury
Estate, Poplar, London, built in 1950–1 to designs by
Frederick Gibberd.*
[Elain Harwood]

Figure 17
*Market Place, Harlow, built in 1955–6 to designs by
Frederick Gibberd. The access road on the right was
closed and the square fully pedestrianised in 1964.*
[AA98/06939]

Other British pedestrian precincts of these early years were small and suburban, so did not influence the town centre at Stevenage – though they did reflect the increasing concern to separate people (especially young children) from vehicles. They included Park Square in the King's Heath area of Northampton (1953–4) and the Willenhall neighbourhood centre in Coventry (1958–9).

This selection of schemes helps to support Leonard Vincent's later comment that 'most architect planners round about 1950 had come to the conclusion that it was a good idea to keep traffic out of shopping centres'.[21] As he went on to emphasise, the earliest results were achieved in areas which had been seriously damaged by wartime bombing, as at Coventry, Exeter and Poplar, and were therefore a priority. The concept of pedestrianisation did not, however, gain wide support among shopkeepers, the managers of multiple stores and many planners. As an approach to planning urban areas it was still highly controversial in the first half of the 1950s, as is well shown by the discussions surrounding the pedestrian town centre at Stevenage.

Development of the pedestrian plan at Stevenage

Following the approval of the Master Plan for Stevenage in early 1950, work proceeded at pace. The task of developing a scheme for the town centre was given to Clifford Holliday as Chief Architect of the Development Corporation. He brought in two main consultants – Professor Gordon Stephenson, who had produced the draft Master Plan in 1946, and through him the American planner Clarence Stein, recruited as a 'second consultant'.[22] Stephenson had studied in the United States where he met his wife, the planner Flora Crockett, and was unusually open to American ideas. By this point, Stein was already a well-known figure in the planning and garden city movement, having made his name internationally with the plan for Radburn, New Jersey (1929–32) – the first neighbourhood in the world to separate traffic and pedestrians. Stevenage Development Corporation considered itself 'fortunate in being able to obtain the advice of so pre-eminent an expert'.[23] In August 1950 Holliday, Stephenson and Stein – the latter based in a pub in Old Stevenage – closeted themselves away to work on a scheme for the town centre. By 5 September they had produced a three-page report outlining the design and function of the site, along with sketch plans of the pedestrian shopping precinct.

At a meeting with the Development Corporation on 20 September, Stephenson explained the proposals in detail, focusing on the pedestrian scheme, the road system and 'the method of bringing both cars and buses to within walking distance of the shops'. He noted that 'These principles were new in Great Britain but they had been adopted in the U.S.A.', and added that he, Holliday and Stein were all 'solidly agreed on the scheme in principle'.[24] Later, Stephenson recalled that 'In presenting the plan, we knew there would be no precedents to cite ... Acceptability was going to be the difficulty. Prejudice stemming from conventional wisdom, inexperience and lack of knowledge would have to be overcome'.[25] A diagrammatic plan of the town centre was produced by Stein in October 1950, and a final, coloured version was produced by Holliday's team in November, following various amendments – including the addition of a road (built as St George's Way) between the town centre and the Town Gardens (Fig. 18).

As the plans and related reports show, the work undertaken by Stephenson, Stein and Holliday was of fundamental influence on Stevenage town centre as built. For instance, the plans indicate what Stephenson described in 1950 as shops 'grouped around a central north-south court, with an east-west pedestrian access group to the south and another to the north', an arrangement which relates closely to the town centre as planned in detail. Stephenson also envisaged 'canopies to afford shelter' – though the suggestion that shops should be of a single storey was subsequently rejected at the behest of the Ministry.[26] Stephenson set out plans for a 'cultural centre including a County College' at the southern end of the shopping precinct, an administrative centre (including a town hall) balancing this at the north, an industrial area and railway station on the west of the Great North Road, and a 'green area' (with buildings such as a church and swimming baths) on the east – all features of the town centre as subsequently constructed. As to cars, these were to be 'left in the parking spaces round the outside of the Centre behind the services entrances, and people will continue on foot to the front of the shops'.[27]

The outline plan for Stevenage's new town centre was accepted in principle by the Development Corporation at the meeting in September 1950 – even though it represented 'a marked departure from current practice'.[28] The scheme was submitted to the Minister of Local Government and Planning in December

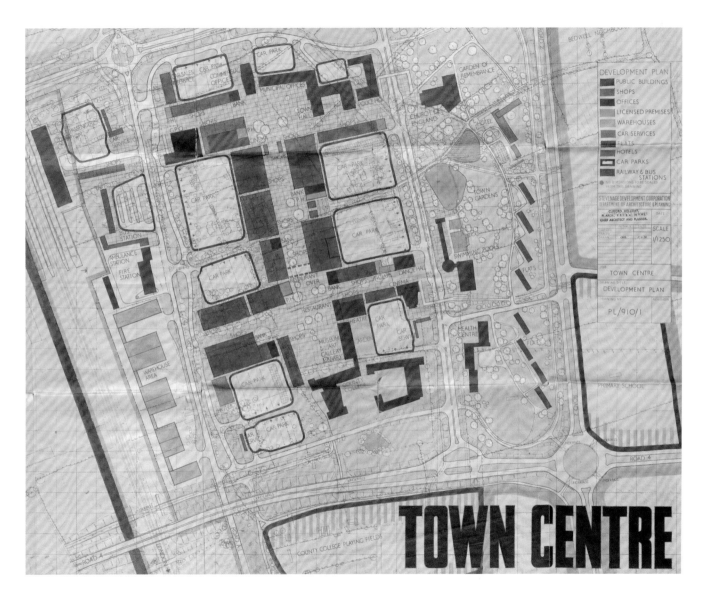

Figure 18
Plan of Stevenage town centre, dated November 1950. This was of significant influence on the town centre plans as finally approved.
[Clarence Stein papers, #3600. Rare and Manuscript Collections, Cornell University Library]

1950. Stein provided advice about the more detailed aspects of the proposal into spring 1951 – the year he published his seminal book *Towards New Towns for America*. Advice was also provided by Brandon Howell (1918–87), a colleague of Stephenson's at Liverpool University, who made a special study of American shopping centres.

The town centre scheme was approved by the Ministry in June 1951, and a more detailed report was submitted by Gordon Stephenson in November 1951. Under the new Chief Architect Donald Reay – who took over from Holliday in March 1952 – the proposals were refined, with a fresh set of plans endorsed in October that year. Stevenage town centre was, therefore, at its detailed design stage at almost exactly the same time as – if not slightly earlier than – the schemes for Coventry's Upper Precinct, the Lijnbaan in Rotterdam and Vällingby in Sweden.

Opposition to a pedestrian plan for Stevenage: 'You can't have a shopping centre without a street'[29]

The path from this point was not clear, however. Various figures remained critical of the proposed pedestrian plan for Stevenage, including officials at the Ministry of Housing and Local Government and members of the Estates Department at the Development Corporation. There was concern that the plan was 'too much of a novelty' and that if the scheme failed, the new town would then have no shopping area of a more conventional type.[30] The retail traders remained especially sceptical, believing that customers preferred to be dropped off at a shop door rather than to approach shops on foot.

A new Chairman of Stevenage Development Corporation – the architect Sir Thomas Bennett (1887–1980), appointed in June 1951 – proved to be an even greater obstacle to the pedestrian scheme. Bennett came from an identical position in Crawley new town, and was from the first very much opposed to a pedestrian town centre for Stevenage. In December 1952 he came out clearly against the proposals, causing 'indignation, if not rage' among many of his fellow Corporation board members.[31] Bennett and others remained worried that a pedestrian shopping precinct was too much of a financial risk.

In March 1953 Reay and his deputy, Leonard Vincent, produced alternative plans showing a pedestrian and vehicular-based shopping centre, and these two options were discussed intensely over the months that followed. Finally, both the Multiple Shops and Retail Distribution Association and the board of Stevenage Development Corporation voted in favour of a dual carriageway through the town centre. In September 1953 the Corporation's architects were asked to produce detailed drawings for the scheme, allowing for conversion of the central road to a pedestrian way at a future date, if desired (Fig. 19). For Donald Reay, who viewed the pedestrian centre as his 'baby', this was an enormous disappointment, and he left the Corporation not long afterwards for a post in the United States, to be succeeded by Leonard Vincent.[32]

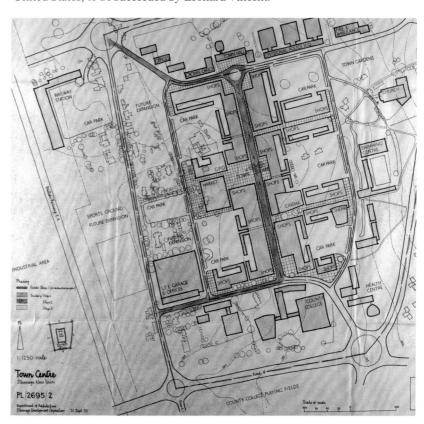

Figure 19
The plan for Stevenage town centre as temporarily reworked in September 1953, incorporating a central road for vehicles.
[HALS, CNT/ST/41/T10, PL2692/2]

However, all was not lost. Support for the revised approach was far from widespread – if anything, the opposite was the case. There was continuing concern among locals about the growth in road accidents and many, including Stevenage Urban District Council, remained in favour of a pedestrian town centre. A new Chairman of the Development Corporation – Sir Roydon Dash (1888–1984), in post from May 1953 – was far more amenable to the pedestrian concept than Bennett had been, though he remained conscious that such planning had 'never been tried in this country on a large scale'.[33] The pressure from locals was intense. The key moment came in January 1954, when a local group including John and Susan Morris of the Stevenage Town Forum organised an open meeting – attended by representatives of the Development Corporation and the Ministry of Housing and Local Government. This passed a unanimous resolution desiring a pedestrian town centre for Stevenage and, following the submission of further evidence, soon the Ministry was convinced.

In April 1954 the Corporation noted that it had 'been compelled to revise its plans for the Town Centre', and the following month Vincent led a group on an exploratory (and successful) visit to see the pedestrian Lijnbaan in Rotterdam.[34] Roydon Dash subsequently noted that if it was possible to make a pedestrian street a success in that city, then it should be even more successful in Stevenage, 'where conditions would be more favourable'.[35] Detailed drawings were with the Ministry shortly afterwards and a new scheme, prepared by Leonard Vincent, was approved in December 1954 – slightly later than those for Coventry and the town centre at Harlow. However, unlike them, it was a completely pedestrian scheme from the first, and claimed with justification to be the first all-pedestrian shopping and administrative centre in the United Kingdom.

The final town centre scheme

Leonard Vincent's team produced detailed drawings and models for Stevenage town centre from 1954 through to 1959 – with an especially intense phase of activity in 1954–6. These were exhibited to the general public at the Ministry's offices in Whitehall in May 1958, and a complete town centre layout plan was produced in December 1959 (Fig. 20). All of the designs built on the work undertaken by Clifford Holliday, Gordon Stephenson and Clarence Stein by setting out a roughly rectangular area with the pedestrian precinct at its core. Around this were to be administrative buildings including a town hall on the north, a bus station, offices and entertainment amenities on the west with the railway station and industrial area beyond, public amenities on the south and leisure buildings with additional offices and a new parish church edging a town park on the east. The town centre area was around 55 acres, with about half of this occupied by the shopping centre. Its scale was consciously chosen to make it 'compact and easily traversed', while the aim overall was 'to create an intimate urban atmosphere reminiscent of some of the older cathedral cities'.[36]

The main component of the shopping precinct was a route running north–south (the future Queensway), about a third of a mile long and 49ft (15m) wide, divided into three unequal lengths and planes. Its orientation was devised to ensure that the distribution of sunlight between the two sides was as equal as

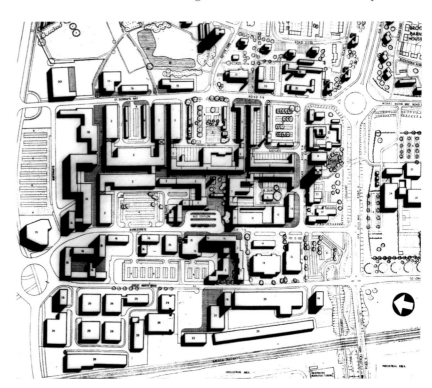

Figure 20
Detailed layout plan for Stevenage town centre,
December 1959.
[Stevenage Museum]

possible. At right angles to this were two shorter and narrower pedestrian ways running east–west – the future Market Place and Park Place. A broader precinct to the north, The Forum, was planned from the beginning but only constructed in the 1970s.

Around its mid-point, Queensway was to open out into the Town Square, at the heart of the new town centre. This continued with an L-shaped block to the north-west, framing the bus station and creating the sense of another, larger square. The bus station was accessed via Danestrete, the only vehicle route which entered the town centre itself. At that time the other roads – Northgate (north), London Road or the old Great North Road (west), Six Hills Way (south) and St George's Way (east) – were planned so as to form the centre's boundaries. The surface car parks serving the commercial core – an integral part of Stevenage's pedestrian planning concept, along with the bus station – were placed on its edges. They were accessed directly from St George's Way and Danestrete, with one of the surface car parks on the east serving as the base for Stevenage's open market. Throughout, the novel concept of pedestrianisation was followed. This meant that every shop had to have a customer entrance from a pedestrian way, but also a goods entrance from a service road at the rear. This practical planning, taking account of access, led to the placing of large retail units at the corners of blocks.

An approach to the form, materials and heights of the buildings in the town centre had been devised by summer 1956, including the use of a module measuring 3ft 4in. (102cm) (*see* p. 51).[37] The area was to be dominated by buildings of no more than three storeys. Taller buildings were placed only at carefully selected sites, where they would make most impact. This is well shown by models of the town centre scheme produced in *c.* 1959 (*see* p. 14). Aside from a couple of four-storey office blocks and the church tower, the only taller buildings shown in the main area are the town hall and administrative buildings at the far north, an office block on the west side of the bus station (the future Daneshill House) and a point block closing the vista south along Queensway ('The Towers'). Later, Leonard Vincent wrote about his intentions in this area:

Differences of height to add architectural interest to the Central Area are produced by buildings on the perimeter, i.e. flats, office blocks, etc. This is the basic concept of the Town Centre design ... The introduction of any structure out of scale with the core would produce a disastrous result, however well it is designed.[38]

The scheme for the Town Square was worked up in 1956–7, with detailed architectural drawings and models produced for the clock tower and the adjacent elevated podium or platform, enclosing public toilets (Figs 21 and 22). Even at this early stage, a piece of sculpture was intended as a major feature of the platform, a long, narrow structure aligned north–south. Also by 1957 there were plans for 'a ceramic panel on one of the main buildings'.[39] These were later realised as the sculpture *Joy Ride* and the tiled mural on the Co-operative supermarket (*see* p. 40 and p. 44).

The designs and models clearly show that landscaping was a vital element of Stevenage town centre from the outset. In order to retain a sense of history, continuity and character, the Development Corporation agreed to incorporate many existing trees into the new streetscape. This innovative approach had been conceived by 1949 and was developed by the consultants Gordon Stephenson

Figure 21
Sketch of the Town Square scheme, produced in c. 1957.
[HALS, Off Acc 793, bundle 14]

and Clarence Stein, along with landscape architect Gordon Patterson. According to Patterson, the existence of mature trees actually led to the choice of siting for the Town Square.[40] The trees were intended to create points of interest, linking old and new, as well as providing shade to shoppers and breaking up the new open spaces.

Leonard Vincent and his team at Stevenage Development Corporation kept close control of the design process. Only in rare instances were buildings designed by different architects. For example, the church was designed for the diocese of St Albans by the firm Seely & Paget, the Hertfordshire County Council structures on the fringes of the town centre were designed by the County Architect's team, and five of the larger shop premises were designed by the in-house architects or preferred consultants of the relevant firms (including Boots and Woolworth's). However, all the structures followed a design ethos set out by Vincent and had to be formally approved by the Corporation before construction could begin.

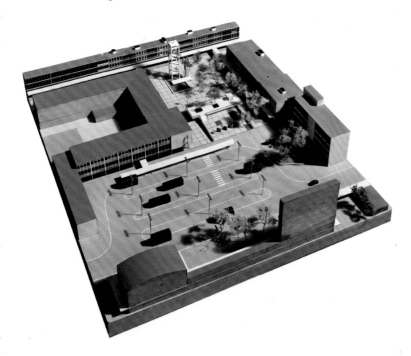

Figure 22
Model of the Town Square and bus station, produced by
Leonard Vincent and his team in 1956.
[Stevenage Museum]

Leonard G. Vincent (1916–2007), Chief Architect of Stevenage new town

The figure who had the greatest influence on the design of Stevenage new town was Leonard Grange Vincent. The son of a postmaster, he was born in 1916 near Seven Kings in Ilford, Essex. He was educated locally at Forest House School, leaving there in 1933 to train as an architect. Vincent studied at the Northern Polytechnic in London, qualifying as both an Associate of the Royal Institute of British Architects (RIBA) and an Associate Member of the Town Planning Institute. However, his career had barely begun when it was interrupted by the Second World War, at which point Vincent joined the Army. He was subsequently commissioned in the Royal Engineers, and reached the rank of major before the war ended.

Leonard Vincent in a photograph taken around the time of Stevenage shopping precinct's completion in 1958. [Courtesy of John Vincent]

Returning to the drawing office after demobilisation, Vincent set up in private practice in Essex. As with others in his profession at that time, his imagination was fired by the prospect of creating new towns, and in 1949 he joined the staff of Stevenage Development Corporation. He initially served as Assistant Chief Architect, working under Clifford Holliday, but was promoted as Deputy Chief Architect in 1952 and then became Chief Architect in 1954, taking over the position from Donald Reay.

It was just at this time that it was finally decided that Stevenage town centre should be planned and built as an all-pedestrian precinct. So it was that the detailed work was undertaken by Leonard Vincent and his team, which included architects such as Raymond Gorbing (1921–2013) and Leslie Aked (1912–84). Vincent had a controlling role throughout, overseeing the work of his colleagues and liaising closely with others who constructed buildings in the town centre, such as Hertfordshire County Council and Stevenage Urban District Council. For his work on the town centre, Vincent was appointed a Commander of the Order of the British Empire (CBE) in 1960 – a rare honour for an architect at that time.

In 1962, given the decline of new design work and an uncertain future for Stevenage Development Corporation, Vincent went into private practice with his colleague Ray Gorbing, with whom he had worked closely since 1950. The firm Vincent & Gorbing, still going strong today, continued to provide architectural design, planning and development advice for Stevenage in the years which followed, though their work also extended beyond this area. Throughout these years, until 1980, Vincent worked as Consultant Architect and Planner to the Corporation, with dedicated offices and a secretary on the fourth floor of Daneshill House, liaising closely with his successors as Chief Architect – Leslie Aked (his former deputy) and Brian Alford (1923–97).

Leonard Vincent lived in Old Stevenage with his wife, Evelyn née Gretton (1918–98), and their children – first at a Development Corporation house, and from 1958 at a house of his own design, Medbury in Rectory Lane. This was his home until his death in 2007, at the age of 93.

4

Realising the proposals for the shopping precinct

It must have been with a great sense of relief and anticipation that Stevenage Development Corporation finally began work on the new town centre in 1954, following approval of the overall scheme that year. The earliest efforts focused on the road network – including Danestrete, the centre's main vehicular road, begun in autumn 1954 – along with the provision of services and the laying out of the site (Fig. 23). In 1955 work began on laying out the bus station half-way up Danestrete, and this was complete by summer 1956. For the next couple of years, until the bus station's formal opening in October 1958, it would serve as the place for drop-off and storage of building materials, as well as for prefabricated construction (Fig. 24).

Building of the town centre was undertaken in phases. First came the shopping precinct, with associated areas such as the Town Square and surrounding surface car parks. Naturally this was the focus, as the Corporation was keen to ensure that the new town could be financially self-sufficient as quickly as possible. Work on the precinct was largely complete by autumn 1958, though construction continued into 1959 and the precinct was only formally opened in that year – the ceremony being performed by the Queen on 20 April 1959. The Corporation retained the freehold of all the property except the church and some public buildings, and only a minority of companies were granted ground leases. This helped to ensure that profits would return to the Corporation and its successors for reinvestment in the town in future years.

The first phase shopping precinct of 1956–9 – 'the famous walking town centre'[41]

Chronology of construction

Work was initiated on the town centre's road network in autumn 1954, but the main building contract began in September 1956 (*see* Appendix). Construction was of two types: a precast reinforced concrete frame for buildings in the Town Square and the major pedestrian streets, with some internal brick walls; and brick cross-wall construction in the 'minor pedestrian ways', Market Place and the south part of Queensway. The plan as outlined in 1951 was to begin at the south end of the town centre development, since this was furthest away from the High Street of Old Stevenage. The approach meant that the latter could

Postcard showing Stevenage Town Square and Queensway in c. 1960.
[Author's collection]

function separately for as long as possible. In reality, work started with the main part of the Town Square, but did generally proceed in a south to north direction.

The first range to be built was what was known as 'block 7' on the south side of the Town Square, including the future Co-operative store. Construction then moved in November 1956 to 'block 9' on the north side of the Town Square and in December to 'block 8' on the east, forming the central section of Queensway. The south part of Queensway (blocks 3 and 4) was initiated in January 1957, and throughout that year work progressed along Market Place (blocks 1 and 2), north up Queensway and into Park Place (the remainder of blocks 8 and 9). In this initial phase of work, construction only reached as far as the junction of Queensway and Park Place. Historic photographs show a rural landscape beyond that point (*see* Fig. 29).

Figure 23
The site of Stevenage new town centre looking west, in a photograph of c. 1955.
[Stevenage Museum]

By summer 1957 the skeleton structures were being given their external cladding and internal dividing walls. Work also started on the remaining part of the Town Square, framing the bus station. This L-shaped block was built in two phases – first the east section (part of block 9), which was constructed in 1957–8, and then the north section (block 10) was built in 1958 (*see* Figs 24 and 35) Shopfitting began in January 1958 with the Co-operative store at the south-east corner of the Town Square. The paving of the pedestrian ways in two shades of grey was largely complete by the middle of that year, and work then started on the canopies above the ground floors of the blocks and also the cross canopies (Fig. 25). The latter were single-storey shelters traversing the pedestrian routes, joining together the canopies of the shops on each side. In 1958, a representative of the Development Corporation noted that the cross canopies 'meet a real need in providing shelter for shoppers in wet weather' (*see* Figs 38 and 46).[42]

Figure 24
Image of 1958 showing construction of the north arm of the Town Square, with the bus station being used for the storage of materials.
[Stevenage Museum]

The Town Square itself was laid out during the first half of 1958, incorporating existing mature trees, and was in use by July. Work on the clock tower and pool was delayed by a London dock strike and only began in August 1958, when work on the adjacent platform was also underway. Due to the lie of the land, the square slopes down from west to east. It was planned as a series of components or areas: the clock tower and pool on the east; the central platform and public toilets, with the upper level overhanging the base to north and south and aligned staircases to east and west; and an open paved area on the west, next to the bus station. Ramped paving on the north and south sides of the square allowed pedestrians to reach Queensway without ascending the stairs of the platform.

The platform and toilets were completed before the clock tower, in the autumn of 1958. *Joy Ride*, a work by the Czech sculptor Franta Belsky (1921–2000) on top of the platform, was unveiled on 29 September of that year. The artist later described the piece, which depicts a mother swinging her small son

Figure 25
Construction of Queensway, looking north in 1958.
[Stevenage Museum]

Figure 26
Joy Ride *by Franta Belsky, unveiled in September 1958.*
[John Maltby/RIBA Collections]

over her back in play, as 'a symbol of the new towns – a happy new town riding on the back of the old' (Fig. 26 and *see* Fig. 127).[43] The height of the platform itself was carefully matched to the surrounding buildings, and it provided a

Figure 27
Postcard of c. 1960 showing the platform in the Town Square, designed to fit in with the surrounding buildings and clock tower.
[Author's collection]

Figure 28
The clock tower in Stevenage's Town Square, unveiled in December 1958.
[DP233263, Derek Kendall]

facility which was both functional and social (Fig. 27 and *see* Fig. 115). By part concealing the Town Square it enticed the pedestrian to explore the sequence of spaces in the town centre. This form of picturesque planning was defined by Thomas Sharp and Hubert de Cronin Hastings in a survey of Oxford in 1947 and made fashionable as 'townscape', a series of studies in the *Architectural Review* (owned by Hastings) mainly by Gordon Cullen.[44]

The clock tower was formally unveiled in December 1958. This precast concrete openwork structure, an iconic feature of Stevenage town centre, was designed by Leonard Vincent and his team 'from a "looking-up" point of view' (Fig. 28).[45] It bears a schematic map of Stevenage new town on its east side, formed out of tiles produced by Carter's of Poole and apparently designed by Vincent himself.[46] On the south side is a plaque unveiled by the Queen in 1959 commemorating the completion of the first phase of the precinct and the naming of Queensway, while a fine bronze of Lewis Silkin by Franta Belsky was added on the west side in 1974 (*see* Fig. 103). The clock tower was placed at the south-east corner of a large, rectangular pool, edged with low brick walls (*see* p. 36). This featured a raised circular fountain on its west side.

Meanwhile, the shops and other business premises in the precinct were completed (Fig. 29). In all, the first phase comprised 108 shops. Strictly speaking, the first to begin trading – on 14 June 1958 – was a branch of Lavells

Figure 29
The north part of Queensway as completed in 1958. At this date, there were no buildings beyond the junction with Park Place.
[© The Francis Frith Collection]

confectioners and tobacconists at 30 Queensway. However, the accolade of being the first (and largest) retail premises to open in Stevenage town centre generally goes to 'Co-operative House', which opened the same day at 6–8 Town Square. This housed the Letchworth, Hitchin and District Co-operative Society; it has since been converted as a branch of Primark. On its main elevation, facing the clock tower, it was decorated with a large ceramic mural (Fig. 30). The work of the Hungarian artist Gyula Bajó or Bajio (1907–84), this symbolises the 'spirit and activities' of the co-operative movement.[47]

Other premises in the area opened during the second half of 1958. These included the Fine Fare supermarket and Davants furniture store on the north

Figure 30
The Co-op, opened in June 1958, with its colourful tiled mural by the artist Gyula Bajó.
[Elain Harwood]

Figure 31
Stevenage Town Square seen at night in 1959, with the Fine Fare supermarket on the corner with Queensway. [Stevenage Museum]

side of the Town Square, opened in October (Fig. 31). At the end of that year, 55 shops were trading in the precinct – over 60 per cent of those built – and three months later the number had risen to 86.[48] Tom Hampson, the Corporation's Social Relations Officer, wrote that 'the mounting excitement of local housewives at each successive shop opening has been a source of much satisfaction to the corporation' (Fig. 32).[49]

In April 1959 the shopping precinct was formally opened by the Queen and by December that year, all of the shops constructed in the first phase had opened, as well as a number of other premises (Fig. 33). These included the Edward the Confessor public house at 1 Town Square, to the north of the bus station (*see* Fig. 49). Also opened at this time was the town centre market, which traded on Fridays and Saturdays on the surface car park between Queensway and St George's Way (Fig. 34). This was accessed through a number of specially designed 'through' shops, including Tesco in Market Place and Sainsbury's in Queensway.

Fundamental to the success of Stevenage town centre's pedestrian scheme was the provision of adequate car parking and public transport. In 1958 one

Figure 32
The lower part of Queensway in 1958 – already
thronging with people, even before the shopping
precinct's official opening.
[RIBA Collections]

Figure 33
The Queen visiting Stevenage to formally open the
shopping precinct on 20 April 1959.
[Stevenage Museum]

Figure 34
From 1959 to 1973, the town centre's open market was
held in Market Square, between Queensway and
St George's Way.
[Stevenage Museum]

journal commented approvingly that 'shoppers leaving buses at the bus station or cars in the car parks have only a few steps to walk to the nearest shop', and bus users did not have to navigate any road crossings.[50] The bus station on the immediate west of the Town Square was formally opened in October 1958, bringing passengers into the heart of the new precinct (Fig. 35). It was served by a bus garage on Danestrete, built by the London Transport Executive (LTE) under Chief Architect Thomas Bilbow (1893–1983). This opened in April 1959, and was the second built by LTE to a new 'streamline' design specially evolved for country areas and for new towns in particular.[51] It had a low office range by the street and a tall garage block behind, capable of accommodating nearly 50 buses (Fig. 36).

The initial aim was to provide parking space for around 2,000 cars, but this figure had been doubled by 1959. The first car parks opened in October 1958 – at Westgate, to the north of the Town Square, and at East Gate, to the south of Market Place. A car park on the west side of Danestrete followed in December 1958, and the Market Square car park east of the precinct was opened in two stages in 1959. Additionally, smaller areas of garaging and car parking were

Figure 35
The bus station, an integral component of the
pedestrian town centre, opened by the Town Square
in October 1958.
[© The Francis Frith Collection]

Figure 36
The bus garage on Danestrete, built in 1957–9 to designs
by the London Transport Executive. It was demolished
in 1993.
[Stevenage Museum]

provided, including The Quadrant, a cul-de-sac car park off Southgate that opened in October 1958. The Market Place car park included a public toilet block, designed in July 1956, while in one corner of the East Gate car park was the boiler house, designed by Vincent and his team in February 1956 and completed in *c*. 1958 (*see* p. 151). This heated some of the larger stores and the precinct's flats. The provision of a single building avoided the need for multiple chimneys, and helped the development meet the requirements of the Clean Air Act of 1956.

Design – unity and variety

The exterior design of Stevenage's shopping precinct was highly modern and, for the time, innovative. This was intentional – Leonard Vincent wrote that 'When the time came to build the centre of the New Town most people hoped for a new approach to design', adding that the architectural profession 'hoped for great things'.[52] There was little of the relevant type and scale to provide inspiration from British developments of the 1940s and early 1950s, apart from the recent Upper Precinct at Coventry – though this still adopted a stripped-down classical style (*see* Fig. 13). Other bombed city centres were being rebuilt in a similarly conservative style, while the shopping centres of developments like the Lansbury Estate in Poplar were much smaller in scale, being more akin to one of Stevenage's neighbourhood centres. In 1959 Vincent stated that 'Generally ... no more than compromises have been offered, presenting too often the disadvantages of the orthodox without the advantages of new thinking'.[53]

In producing the detailed designs for Stevenage town centre it was natural, therefore, that Vincent and his colleagues at the Development Corporation looked further afield. Their models were the recently completed developments at the Lijnbaan in Rotterdam – visited by Vincent and others from the Corporation and Council in May 1954 – and Vällingby near Stockholm (*see* Figs 11 and 12). On the completion of Stevenage's shopping precinct, the press commented that some locals had recently visited Lijnbaan and had been 'amazed at the similarity to Stevenage' (Figs 37 and 38).[54]

One of the most notable aspects of the design and planning of Stevenage town centre is its unity, producing what was termed at the time a 'planner's dream'.[55] In detailed planning as in reality, it was the vision of Leonard Vincent and his colleagues – with Raymond Gorbing architect-in-charge of the first phase. Furthermore, the shopping precinct was built under a single contract by

one main contractor – the firm Harry Neal Ltd. Throughout, unity and
consistency was the major aim, and this was aided by a comparatively brief
programme of construction. Victor Stallabrass, Chief Estate Officer at the
Development Corporation, noted in 1959 that 'It must be very rare that a project
for a shopping centre as large as the Stevenage Town Centre is carried through
in one stage of building'.[56]

Vincent set out a clear design ethos that extended to the elevations and
height of the buildings, their materials and landscaping. This guided his own
team as well as the work undertaken by others, on the rare occasions where
companies were permitted to use their own architects. This approach was taken
by the Co-operative Society and the so-called 'big five' multiples: W. H. Smith's,
Boots, Sainsbury's, Woolworth's and Dolcis. Designs once submitted were
adapted to conform to Vincent's modular ethos and had to be formally approved
by the Corporation's Planning Committee, while construction was timed to fit in
with the overall schedule of works.

Leonard Vincent and his team clearly studied recent developments in design
and construction when formulating an approach to Stevenage town centre. They
would have been aware, for instance, that the rebuilding of the 'blitzed cities',
beginning with Plymouth but also including Bristol and Coventry, had drawn a
lukewarm response from the architectural press – notably in a series of articles
published in the *Architects' Journal* in late 1952. There was particular criticism
of the lack of unity in the rebuilt urban areas, even though the steel or concrete
frame represented a common factor. D. Rigby Childs and Colin Boyne made the
following suggestion with regard to Bristol:

> This structural element in almost every instance has been disguised, or
> obscured, but nevertheless is there. Might not this, then, provide a solution for
> obtaining unity in the street? Let the City Corporation erect the structural

frame – preferably on a module – for the whole, or part, of a street, and let each shop lease the number of bays it requires and fill in the floors and roof, and within the concrete frame, design its own, brazenly self-advertising façade. Then, however discordant the elements, they would be partially disciplined by the repetitive three-dimensional pattern of the frame.[57]

This is precisely the approach that Vincent and his team took at Stevenage, and it proved to be the one new town centre where this stratagem was adopted – because, unlike Harlow and later new towns, the Development Corporation's architectural team controlled the whole design. Under Vincent, a 3ft 4in. (102cm) module was developed for most of the town centre precinct, within a larger 20ft (6.1m) grid, with shop frontages varying from 20ft to 120ft (36.6m) – 20ft was standard – and methods of construction being identical. Projecting canopies above the ground-floor shopfronts were a consistent feature throughout, along with the single-storey cross canopies traversing the pedestrian ways. The resulting effect can best be seen in Queensway, where the multiple retailers were based.

Figure 39
The east side of Queenway showing the unified design of the precinct's external architecture, based on a grid module.
[DP275704, James O. Davies]

Even though some of these firms designed their own premises, there was no inconsistency of design, apart from signage and small details (Fig. 39).

The constructional approach taken at Stevenage was made possible by technical advances of the early 1950s. The year 1952 had seen the breakthrough made in curtain-walled office design with the building of Lever House in New York by Gordon Bunshaft of Skidmore, Owings & Merrill. A uniform grid across the entire façade, infilled with glass, timber or composite panels, offered a light, well-scrubbed image appropriate for a company manufacturing soap products. The form was quickly adopted by other firms wanting to appear progressive. Large areas of glass, sometimes without risers or fascias, were beginning to dominate the most progressive storefronts – led in Britain by the chain of Dolcis shoe shops erected to the designs of Ellis E. Somake (1908–98), whose work included the Stevenage store.

Bringing these elements together to provide a minimal backdrop for the latest in display techniques was a logical next step, made possible by the rapid development of aluminium and glass curtain walling in Britain in the years 1955–7. The *Architectural Review* demonstrated this new development in a series of articles. In May 1957 – while Stevenage town centre was under construction – it devoted a whole issue to 'Machine-Made America', showing how curtain walling had swept the United States, and followed it in September by 'Walls off the Peg', a substantial report on British systems, some of which were already being exported to North America and Europe.[58] The 1950s and early 1960s buildings of Stevenage town centre are therefore very much of their time, and were in several respects novel in their design and construction in terms of a British context.

Vincent and his team used a set range of materials for the town centre buildings, another means of achieving consistency. Materials, including facings, were chosen to keep maintenance to a minimum; these included steel, glass, stone, brick and mosaic. All the canopies were formed from concrete and steel cantilevers, but were finished in timber. The curtain walls of the main blocks, such as those in the central part of Queensway, had precast concrete mullions with Portland stone aggregate and galvanised steel windows supplied by Crittalls, the leaders in the field. A company advertisement of 1959, quoting Leonard Vincent, stated proudly that

> Stevenage new town is remarkable for many things and perhaps not least
> for the fact that Crittall windows are installed in over half the buildings in

the area. Almost all the town centre buildings, half the factories in the industrial area and most of the houses in the town ... have Crittall windows. And they are windows that have been *positively rustproofed* by the hot-dip galvanizing process, which means less maintenance costs.[59]

The approach taken by Stevenage Development Corporation was also innovative with regard to signage and advertising. It produced a comprehensive scheme for outdoor 'advertisements' – prepared largely by Ian M. Purdy, working under Leonard Vincent. This included areas such as illuminated signs, 'brightness zoning' at night, directional and hanging signs under the canopies, the lettering used for names of stores and even the placement of such lettering on the façades (Fig. 40). This was believed to be the earliest of its kind in Britain – Vincent wrote that it was 'probably the first time that a positive approach has been made

Figure 40
The imaginative approach taken to signage, lighting and advertising in Stevenage inspired this drawing by Kenneth Browne, published in 1957.
[Architectural Review]

Figure 41
Market Place in 1963, looking east towards the church. The whole ensemble, including street furniture, was designed by Leonard Vincent's team at Stevenage Development Corporation.
[Stevenage Museum]

to outdoor advertising with the object of integrating it with architectural design'.[60] The approach had a national impact, being said to deserve 'high praise' by Kenneth Browne, writing in the *Architectural Review* in August 1957.[61] Vincent and his team also designed all the town centre's street furniture, including lamp standards, special post boxes, concrete flower planters and 'bike parks' placed at the centre of the shopping ways (Fig. 41).

Stevenage Development Corporation took a proactive approach to sculpture and external decoration, providing key points of interest throughout the town centre. Whereas at Harlow a separate arts trust was formed, at Stevenage the Corporation itself took on the work of commissioning, often favouring local artists. In the first phase, there were two major commissions: the bronze sculpture *Joy Ride* by Franta Belsky, placed atop the platform in the Town Square in 1958; and the tiled mural of 1958 by Gyula Bajó, also in the Town Square (*see* Figs 26 and 30). Slightly later in date was the aluminium wall sculpture by Peter Lyon (b. 1926) of Birmingham, erected in 1964 on the west face of Davants at 21–23 Town Square, overlooking the bus station (Fig. 42).

The overall cohesion of the shopping precinct was commented upon, not least by Leonard Vincent, who wrote a series of articles around the time of its

Figure 42
View looking north-east across the Town Square in
1970. In the left foreground is the wall sculpture by
Peter Lyon erected in 1964.
[Stevenage Museum]

completion. In 1959 he stated proudly, 'The Centre is a complex of buildings forming a coherent architectural conception, as well as meeting the needs of numerous tenants or building lessees'.[62] However, Vincent and his team happily seized upon opportunities for variety. Most buildings in the town centre were dominated by plain runs of glazing with concrete aggregate beneath, but some in Queensway had coloured panels – variously red, blue, yellow, black and white, giving a 'gay and eye-catching' appearance to the town centre (*see* Fig. 116).[63] On the upper floors of Woolworth's facing onto the Town Square, the red-coloured panels were decorated with Ws, both at first- and second-floor level. Primary colours were also introduced into some glazing – for instance, in the side windows of the first-floor flats in Market Place.

Exposed brickwork was similarly used to provide variety and interest and to draw together disparate buildings of the town centre. In particular, a specific design approach was consciously taken for the buildings of the minor pedestrian ways, Market Place and lower Queensway, expressing their place within the overall hierarchy of the precinct. Here, buildings were predominantly of brick, with infill panels of steel and glass and prominent upper-floor balconies or bay windows (Fig. 43). The two minor pedestrian ways were further united by their

Figure 43
*The lower part of Queensway, looking south towards
The Towers, a residential point block built in 1960–3.*
[DP233323, Derek Kendall]

Figure 44
*Blank walls such as this – faced with Kentish flint
aggregate panels – helped to provide variety and
contrast in the town centre.*
[Stevenage Museum]

placing within the townscape – the outer vista of each was closed by a tall structure, the tower of the church for Market Place and The Towers point block for Queensway, a design approach also used at developments including the Lijnbaan.

Another design component was the blank walls in the town centre, often at the ends of blocks. These were faced variously in brickwork, render or precast aggregate and Kentish flint. The aggregate-faced walls were often incised with lines forming a grid, as at the junction of Queensway and Market Place (Fig. 44). It was these blank walls that were often used for the display of decoration or sculpture, or prominent lettering – such as the illuminated lettering bearing the name of Fine Fare on the store's south side, placed on a mosaic ground (*see* p. 110).

There was a deliberate aim to achieve interest in the town centre's layout, following picturesque principles. This was not simply linear; instead, the pedestrian ways were broken up by changes of plane – most notably, the dog-leg where Queensway joins Market Place (Fig. 45). Another key objective was the creation of a sense of intimacy. Tom Hampson of the Development Corporation wrote that the 'feeling of intimacy and enclosure as opposed to one of coldness and draughtiness' was achieved by 'a careful relation of heights of buildings to

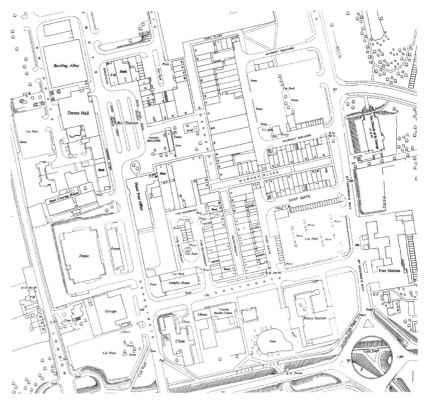

Figure 45
Ordnance Survey map depicting the central area of
Stevenage in 1963.

Figure 46
The cross canopy at the south end of Queensway in
1959.
[John Maltby/RIBA Collections]

widths of spaces opposite', while the Corporation's landscape architect Gordon Patterson spoke about the interplay of 'constricted' areas and 'broader openings', which helped to avoid dullness.[64] The precinct's cross canopies had a major part to play in achieving this effect, providing brief moments of enclosure as well as shelter (Fig. 46).

The Development Corporation made less attempt to assert control over the actual shopfronts. Leonard Vincent wrote that

> canopies emphasise and unify the architecture in a dramatic manner, so that there is less need to control shopfronts. Shopfronts have, within reason, been allowed freedom, and generally a high standard has been achieved.[65]

There was even greater independence of design with regard to shop interiors. Victor Stallabrass commented that

> It was decided at the outset that the work of the main contractor must be kept as straightforward as possible, so as to minimise the number of variations once construction had begun. For this reason, all the internal finishes of the shops were left to the tenants, who were thus free to design these to meet their individual needs.[66]

Larger shops were carefully planned so they fitted in with the general scheme, while smaller shops were designed to three or four standard sizes so that sufficient choice was given for lessees in the various trades.

Character and typology

The shopping precinct's occupants were depicted in a 1958 plan of the town centre (Fig. 47), but more businesses moved in during the following year. Stevenage Development Corporation pursued a lettings policy for the town centre to create and maintain a 'proper balance' of shop types, traders and uses, all carefully distributed throughout the precinct.[67] Writing in 1959, Victor Stallabrass summarised that the centre comprised, in addition to banks: three department or variety stores; 19 food shops; 27 clothing shops; 14 furnishing, hardware and household goods stores; 6 radio and television stores; 5 newsagents/tobacconists; and 22 miscellaneous shops, including two bookshops

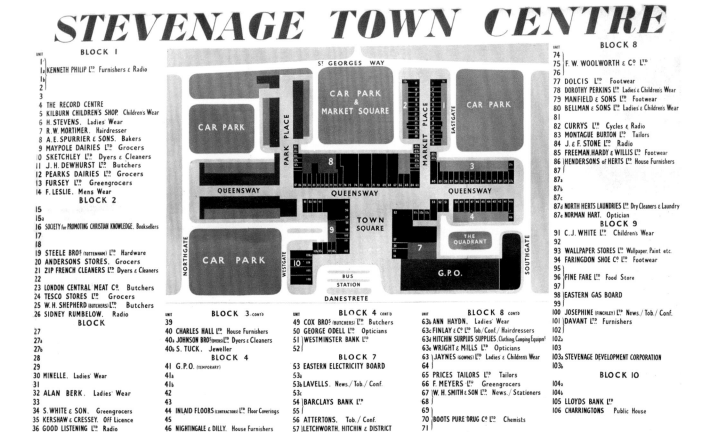

STEVENAGE TOWN CENTRE

BLOCK 1
UNIT
1
1a KENNETH PHILIP LTD. Furnishers & Radio
1b
2
3
4 THE RECORD CENTRE
5 KILBURN CHILDREN'S SHOP. Children's Wear
6 H. STEVENS. Ladies' Wear
7 R.W. MORTIMER. Hairdresser
8 A.E. SPURRIER & SONS. Bakers
9 MAYPOLE DAIRIES LTD. Grocers
10 SKETCHLEY LTD. Dyers & Cleaners
11 J.H. DEWHURST LTD. Butchers
12 PEARKS DAIRIES LTD. Grocers
13 FURSEY LTD. Greengrocers
14 F. LESLIE. Mens' Wear
BLOCK 2
15
15a
16 SOCIETY for PROMOTING CHRISTIAN KNOWLEDGE. Booksellers
17
18
19 STEELE BROS (TOTTENHAM) LTD. Hardware
20 ANDERSONS STORES. Grocers
21 ZIP FRENCH CLEANERS LTD. Dyers & Cleaners
22
23 LONDON CENTRAL MEAT CO. Butchers
24 TESCO STORES LTD. Grocers
25 W.H. SHEPHERD (BUTCHERS) LTD. Butchers
26 SIDNEY RUMBELOW. Radio
BLOCK
27
27a
27b
28
29
30 MINELLE. Ladies' Wear
31
32 ALAN BERK. Ladies' Wear
33
34 S. WHITE & SON. Greengrocers
35 KERSHAW & CRESSEY. Off Licence
36 GOOD LISTENING LTD. Radio
37 PEARCE (HARLOW) LTD. Bakers
38 FORBUOYS LTD. News./Tob./Conf.

BLOCK 3 CONTD
39
40 CHARLES HALL LTD. House Furnishers
40a JOHNSON BROS (DYERS) LTD. Dyers & Cleaners
40b S. TUCK. Jeweller
BLOCK 4
41 G.P.O. (TEMPORARY)
41a
41b
42
43
44 INLAID FLOORS (CONTRACTORS) LTD. Floor Coverings
45
46 NIGHTINGALE & DILLY. House Furnishers
47 GODFREY'S Ladies' Wear
48 BRADLEYS (CHESTER) LTD. Men's Outfitters

BLOCK 4 CONTD
49 COX BROS (BUTCHERS) LTD. Butchers
50 GEORGE ODELL LTD. Opticians
51 WESTMINSTER BANK LTD.
52
BLOCK 7
53 EASTERN ELECTRICITY BOARD
53a
53b LAVELLS. News./Tob./Conf.
53c
54 BARCLAYS BANK LTD.
55
56 ATTERTONS. Tob./Conf.
57 LETCHWORTH, HITCHIN & DISTRICT
62 CO-OPERATIVE SOCIETY LTD.
63a ATTERTONS. Prams, Sports Goods

BLOCK 8 CONTD
63b ANN HAYDN. Ladies' Wear
63c FINLAY & CO LTD. Tob./Conf./Hairdressers
63d HITCHIN SURPLUS SUPPLIES. Clothing, Camping Equipmt
63e WRIGHT & MILLS LTD. Opticians
63 JAYNES (GOWNS) LTD. Ladies & Children's Wear
64
65 PRICES TAILORS LTD. Tailors
66 F. MEYERS LTD. Greengrocers
67 W.H. SMITH & SON LTD. News./Stationers
68
69
70 BOOTS PURE DRUG CO LTD. Chemists
71
72 J. SAINSBURY LTD. Grocers
73

BLOCK 8
UNIT
74
75 F.W. WOOLWORTH & CO LTD.
76
77 DOLCIS LTD. Footwear
78 DOROTHY PERKINS LTD. Ladies & Children's Wear
79 MANFIELD & SONS LTD. Footwear
80 BELLMAN & SONS LTD. Ladies & Children's Wear
81
82 CURRYS LTD. Cycles & Radio
83 MONTAGUE BURTON LTD. Tailors
84 J. & F. STONE LTD. Radio
85 FREEMAN.HARDY & WILLIS LTD. Footwear
86 HENDERSONS of HERTS LTD. House Furnishers
87
87a
87b
87c
87d NORTH HERTS LAUNDRIES LTD. Dry Cleaners & Laundry
87e NORMAN HART. Optician
BLOCK 9
91 C.J. WHITE LTD. Children's Wear
92
93 WALLPAPER STORES LTD. Wallpaper, Paint etc.
94 FARINGDON SHOE CO LTD. Footwear
95
96 FINE FARE LTD. Food Store
97
98 EASTERN GAS BOARD
99
100 JOSEPHINE (FINCHLEY) LTD. News./Tob./Conf.
101 DAVANT LTD. Furnishers
102
102a
103
103a STEVENAGE DEVELOPMENT CORPORATION
103b
BLOCK 10
104a
104b
105 LLOYDS BANK LTD.
106 CHARRINGTONS. Public House

Figure 47
Plan of Stevenage town centre in 1958. The precinct was not complete at this point and some of the premises were not yet occupied.
[Stevenage Museum]

and one specialising in gramophone records and music instruments. There were also three cafés and four hairdressers.[68]

Following a direction from the Ministry of Housing and Local Government in 1953, it was the Corporation's policy to position the major retailers in and directly adjacent to the Town Square, at the heart of the shopping precinct. The largest store was occupied by the Co-op at 6–8 Town Square (*see* Fig. 1), while opposite was a branch of Fine Fare, a supermarket chain established in Welwyn Garden

City in 1951; it grew to rival companies such as Tesco and Sainsbury's before being sold and disappearing in the late 1980s. In addition to its large ground-floor shop area, the Stevenage branch had a popular first-floor café with a balcony overlooking the Town Square (*see* p. 110). Immediately to the east, forming part of Queensway, was a huddle of national multiple retailers including W. H. Smith (at 39–41 Queensway), Boots (at nos 43–45), Sainsbury's (at nos 47–49) and Woolworth's (at nos 51–55) – the last mentioned was in the most visible location of all, facing the clock tower (*see* p. 36). Close by were other chain stores including Dolcis (at 57 Queensway), Dorothy Perkins (at no. 59), Currys (at no. 67), Montague Burton's (at no. 69) and Freeman, Hardy & Willis (at no. 73).

But the national companies were not only located in Queensway. There was a Tesco supermarket at 17 Market Place (*see* Fig. 108), a branch of Rumbelows, the electronic retailer, two doors away, and branches of Sketchley dry cleaners and Maypole Dairies roughly opposite. In terms of public services, there was an Eastern Electricity Board showroom prominently situated at 60 Queensway – at the junction with Market Place (*see* Fig. 44) – and an Eastern Gas Board showroom on the immediate west of Fine Fare. Otherwise, shops in the town centre were mainly run by local and regional firms, including hairdressers, hardware stores, grocers, butchers, clothes shops and bookshops attracted from the old town (Fig. 48). Some of these occupied large and prominent premises, as with Davants furniture shop at 21–23 Town Square, opened in October 1958. On its south side, this was given two highly glazed upper floors supported on four slender pilotis (*see* Fig. 27).

The town centre as completed in 1958–9 also included two banks: a Lloyds opened in July 1958 at 3–5 Town Square and a Barclays opened in September the same year at 2–4 Town Square. Slightly later a branch of Westminster Bank opened at 24–26 Queensway, while the other two major banking firms – Midland and National Provincial – had opened premises in the town centre by the end of 1961. These banks opted 'not to be grouped together but to be dispersed among the shops', and Barclays was given the first choice of location – selecting a prominent position between Co-operative House and the Head Post Office.[69]

Cafés and restaurants were concentrated in the north-west arm of the Town Square, embracing the bus station, making them easily accessible for travellers and convenient as meeting places. They included the Highflier café and the

Figure 48
A view of 1959 illustrating the range of shops and
shopfronts in Queensway.
[Stevenage Museum]

Gatehouse restaurant, while at 1 Town Square – on the corner of Danestrete – was the Edward the Confessor pub, run by Charrington's (Fig. 49). This featured bars and a restaurant, and was the only pub in the area until the opening of the Long Ship at Southgate House in 1966. Such premises fulfilled the vision for the town plan, which placed entertainment buildings towards the west of the centre, though there was also a café ('Coffee Cabin') at the south end of Queensway, by Southgate.

As completed in 1959, the upper floors of the precinct's blocks provided 50,000 sq. ft (4,645m²) of accommodation, which was put to a variety of commercial uses. Over the largest retailers in Queensway and the Town Square, it was common practice for the upper floors to be used for shop storage and staff rooms. Elsewhere, upper floors were used for professional purposes – as the offices of solicitors, accountants, insurance companies and so forth. Some were grouped into 'chambers' for separate letting.

There were also 53 flats and maisonettes on the upper floors in Market Place and the south end of Queensway. These were seen as a means of preventing the

Figure 49
Charrington's Edward the Confessor pub at 1 Town Square, opened in autumn 1959.
[Courtesy of the National Brewery Centre]

Figure 50
The rear of the south blocks of Market Place seen from the East Gate car park, with a 'through-way' and cross canopy at the centre.
[DP278108, Patricia Payne]

centre from becoming 'dead' outside shopping hours. They were intended to provide housing for families, but were also made available to the managers and assistants who worked in the shops below. In 1959 Victor Stallabrass noted that

> The living accommodation has, in nearly every case, been leased with the shop. The Corporation's policy has been to let the shops (or in a few cases the shop sites) direct to the trader who will actually occupy the premises, and not to grant leases to investment companies.[70]

Service access to both shops and the floors above was from the rear of the commercial blocks, via ground-floor entrances and external staircases – many of them reached from the surface car parks (Fig. 50). In cases where upper-floor accommodation was let with a ground-floor shop, it still had its own separate access.

Shopping precinct extensions, 1962–4

Plans for the expansion of Stevenage's shopping precinct were already in hand by the late 1950s. This reflected both its phenomenal early success and revised population figures for the new town – in 1958 the Minister of Housing and Local Government proposed that the ultimate population target should be increased to 80,000, up 20,000 from the original estimate, and this was agreed in 1959. The intention was that new buildings would link the first stage of the precinct with the administrative complex due to be constructed at The Forum (*see* Fig. 20). The popularity of the town centre had confirmed that further commercial premises were urgently required. In spring 1959 an official of the Development Corporation commented that 'Already the waiting list is growing of traders wanting to take shops in the second part of the Centre, including a number of the present lessees of the first part who would like to take larger premises so as to extend their business'.[71]

Detailed design work for 'phase II' of the shopping precinct was undertaken by Leonard Vincent and his team in February and March 1961, and detailed designs for the town hall and administrative complex were prepared in summer that year (Fig. 51). In layout and form, the new work was to follow the principles of the first stage and was 'carefully related to the arrangement and levels of the existing pedestrian ways and shopping blocks'.[72] The Ministry advanced the funds for the scheme in May 1961 and site work began around that time, focusing on the area at the junction of Queensway and Park Place (*see* Fig. 57).

Work on the north part of Queensway was due to start in early 1963, with the town hall and administrative complex set for completion by spring that year. When in July 1961 the government called for economies in public expenditure, some aspects of work on the new town were halted or slowed, though only temporarily. In late 1961 the Development Corporation was emphasising its intention to build a town hall and associated buildings 'as soon as the Government's squeeze on capital expenditure is off'.[73] However, the government's 'bombshell' decision to reconsider the future size and population of Stevenage new town – announced in July 1962 – changed everything.[74] The proposals set out a future population of 150,000, nearly 50 per cent greater than the 80,000 predicted by the current Master Plan. While the Corporation assessed the viability of the proposals, it decided to suspend further planning of development at the north of the town centre pending various investigations – including the possibility of reusing the area allocated to the town hall for additional shops. Ultimately, as will be seen, plans for a dedicated town hall were abandoned altogether, and the construction of the north part of Queensway only took place in the last years of the 1960s, once plans for a greatly expanded new town had been shelved.

Thankfully, some enlargement of the shopping precinct did proceed in the early 1960s. Construction went ahead in two stages from summer 1962 (*see* Fig. 82). First Queensway was extended to the north, the new buildings on

Figure 51
The proposed elevations of the town hall at the north end of Queensway, in a drawing of July 1961. Stevenage Council was critical of the modern form of Leonard Vincent's proposals, which were never executed.
[HALS, Off Acc 793, bundle 36, no. 7]

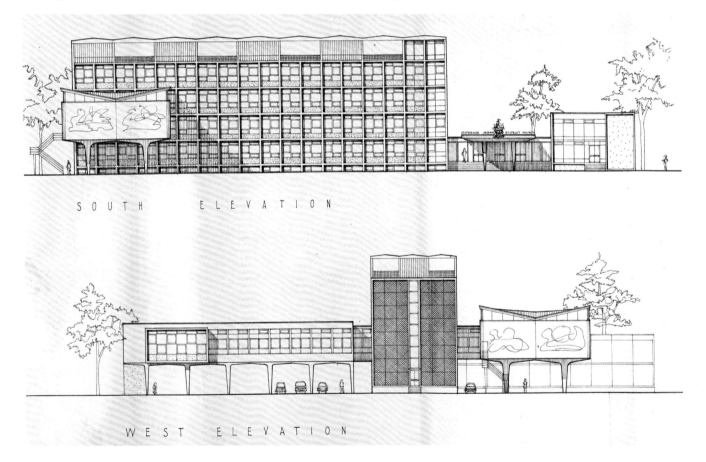

S O U T H   E L E V A T I O N

W E S T   E L E V A T I O N

the west side (nos 48–64) providing shops on the ground floor and commercial space above, with a 'through-way' connecting to the Westgate car park. In design, this new block – largely complete by Christmas 1963 – was virtually identical to the first phase; even the new area of decorative black tilework followed the approach taken earlier with regard to blank walls (Fig. 52).

This range culminated in a new two-storey steel and glass bridge, crossing Queensway on an east–west alignment. In concept, this was similar to the cross canopies built elsewhere in the precinct in providing a partial interruption to the vista on picturesque principles, inviting shoppers to explore further. Stein and Stephenson had included such a bridge in their scheme of 1950. The bridge was sufficiently large to include functional space. The first floor was opened as a Chinese restaurant in May 1964, while on the second level was the Clarion Club – the social headquarters of the Stevenage Labour Party, officially opened in February 1964. Together with the bridge, the most notable aspect of this phase of works was Littlewoods at 77–79 Queensway, on the corner of Queensway and Park Place (Fig. 53). This three-storey building opened in October 1963 and seems to have been designed by Littlewoods' chosen architects; it included sales

Figure 52
The Queensway block of 1962–4 (with yellow panels)
adjoining the 1950s work to the south. The entrance to
the Westgate shopping centre was added in c. 1988.
[DP275705, James O. Davies]

space with a self-service cafeteria on the ground floor. The open area in front of the store, which was set with mature trees, came to be known as 'Littlewoods Square'.

From 1963, as the second stage of 'phase II', Park Place was extended eastwards to St George's Way, with work complete by the end of 1964. It included 22 shops with 20,000 sq. ft (1,858m²) of office space above, as well as flats and maisonettes. Larger-than-standard shop units were provided, designed to accommodate those companies who had booked sites by The Forum only to find this scheme postponed. In design, the Park Place blocks were simpler and plainer than the earlier work in Queensway, but retained the general design ethos (Fig. 54). For instance, they had canopies above the ground floor and were of three storeys, with opaque panels beneath the windows. Open through-ways were included, enabling pedestrians to access the adjacent surface car parks, as were cross canopies.

Figure 53
Littlewoods Square in 2020, with the former Littlewoods store at the centre and the two-storey bridge on the left. Public realm works were completed in this area in 2017.
[DP275708, James O. Davies]

Figure 54
The early 1960s blocks of Park Place, looking west towards Queensway. Cross canopies in this area were removed in 2017.
[DP278905, Patricia Payne]

By the end of 1964, the extension was complete. The press reported a 'bumper Christmas' that year, and in 1965 a survey showed that 20,000–30,000 people visited the town centre on a Saturday – more than a quarter coming from the surrounding region.[75] The rising visitor numbers and increased population figures for the new town would lead to further extensions of the shopping precinct in the later part of that decade and into the 1970s (*see* Chapter 6).

5

Town centre amenities, 1958–65 – building for work, entertainment and leisure

The pedestrian shopping precinct was only one aspect of the plans for Stevenage town centre prepared during the 1950s. In order to function fully, independently and successfully, the centre also needed a wide range of other buildings and amenities. These were first sketched out by Clifford Holliday, Gordon Stephenson and Clarence Stein in 1950, and were included in the plan approved in November that year (*see* Fig. 18).

Buildings such as the church, offices, swimming pool and police station remained a key part of the town centre as planned in detail by Leonard Vincent and his team. For Vincent as for his predecessors, these structures were best grouped into particular 'zones'. The vision had long been that the administrative complex at the north of Queensway (including the town hall) would be balanced by a 'county' complex at the south, on the island of land between Southgate and Six Hills Way (Fig. 55 and *see* Fig. 20). This was to extend to the east, with further 'Crown' and office buildings along the far side of St George's Way. Meanwhile, offices were clustered on the west side of the town centre, close to the railway line and industrial area. Entertainment and leisure buildings were also to be located in this part of the town centre and along a strip of land between St George's Way and the Town Centre Gardens. On the whole, this is how it worked out in practice – though the abandonment in 1966 of plans for a civic centre at the north of Queensway led to certain adjustments.

The design work for the first wave of 'fringe' buildings was undertaken in phases between *c.* 1956 and 1963. Unity and consistency across the whole town centre – both of form and materials – was again a major objective in a bid to avoid a 'disjointed, uncoordinated appearance'.[76] Surviving letters reveal that Vincent's striving for unity of design was consistent and enduring, and was one of the elements of Stevenage that he felt provided the foundation for its international reputation. Just one instance is his stipulation that buildings constructed by anyone other than the Corporation should have open boundaries, the danger being that if each was fenced, 'the effect will be to lose the unity of the Town Centre'.[77] In particular, Vincent fiercely protected his belief that the town centre buildings should generally be no higher than three storeys, except on key sites.

An order of priority for construction placed first St George's Church and then offices, followed closely by public amenities such as the library and by entertainment and leisure facilities. Had the expansion plans not disrupted the

View along Southgate in 2020, showing buildings including the library and health centre (1959–60) and Southgate House (1963–4).
[DP278110, Patricia Payne]

STEVENAGE TOWN CENTRE

Cinema

Town Hall

Law Courts

Railway Station

Hotel

Figure 55
Town centre layout plan produced in November 1965 (north is at the top). At this point, it was still the intention to build a town hall at the north end of Queensway.
[HALS, CNT/ST/15/4/17]

Figure 56
Town Centre Gardens were created in 1958–61 on the east of St George's Way as a 'buffer' between the shopping precinct and the housing beyond.
[DP278141, Patricia Payne]

scheme for the civic centre, this would have been built as part of these works along with art gallery, museum and law courts (*see* Fig. 51). Also built at this time was the County College (1959–61), slightly beyond the town centre to the south. On the east boundary of the town centre another important facility was created: Town Centre Gardens (also known as Town Gardens). This 12-acre site was begun in late summer 1958, planted in spring 1959 and completed in summer 1961 (Fig. 56).

By 1965 the key 'fringe' buildings had been completed, and were said to have made an 'enormous difference' to the town centre's appearance, as well as bringing more people into the area at all times of day (Fig. 57).[78] Only a handful of other amenities followed later – such as the magistrates' court (built to the west of Danestrete in 1972–3), the office block known as Manulife House (built in St George's Way in 1972–3), the ABC cinema (opened 1973) and the arts and leisure centre by the new railway station (1974–5).

Figure 57
Aerial view of 1962 looking north, with Southgate at the bottom and construction beginning on the precinct extension at the top. Various 'fringe' buildings are also shown under construction, including Swingate House (top left) and the swimming pool (top right).
[Stevenage Museum]

Town centre offices

Once work on the shopping precinct was well underway, Stevenage Development Corporation was able to shift its attention to the buildings around the 'core'. Understandably, the construction of offices was a particular focus. This reflected the Corporation's desire to attract a range of both employers and workers to the new town, to encourage companies to move out of London, and to provide jobs for the large cohort of teenagers set to leave school in the coming years.

The first three office buildings constructed were similar in design and close to the Town Square. These were the Head Post Office (built in 1958–9), Langley House (1959–60) and Daneshill House (1959–61). All were designed by Leonard Vincent and his team, though the Post Office was commissioned by the Ministry of Works. To ensure consistency across the whole town centre, the offices used similar materials. For instance, the west elevation of Langley House had a section of wall faced in exposed aggregate panels, incised with lines, while Daneshill House had a panel of decorative tilework on its south façade. In plan, all three offices were composed of simple rectangles with corner staircases, while their elevations drew upon the treatment devised for the shopping precinct: the Post Office and Daneshill House had prominent canopies above the ground floor and all three made use of the modular grid form. However, a more extensive use was made of curtain-walled glazing, provided by Crittalls, ensuring that the spaces within were light and airy. As in the precinct, colour was incorporated to provide interest and distinctiveness. Panels beneath the windows were made

Figure 58
Daneshill House (right) and the Head Post Office (left) seen in a 1980s photograph, looking south across the bus station.
[HALS, CV350]

opaque by infill behind the glass – blue at the Head Post Office, golden yellow at Daneshill House and a mix of pale yellow and blue-grey at Langley House (Fig. 58 and *see* p. 92).

For some time, it had been the intention that the office block on the west of the bus station would be relatively tall. As completed, Daneshill House rose through seven storeys, boasting 19,200 sq. ft (1,784m²) of office space, and was at the time of its completion the highest building in the area (Fig. 59). As well as being prominent, it was of particular significance to the town. Daneshill House was built as the headquarters of Stevenage Development Corporation, and it is clear that Vincent took particular pains over its design, which was in hand from spring 1957. The Corporation staff moved into their new offices in January 1961 – transferring to the heart of the new town from their previous base at Aston House, four miles away.

Figure 59
Daneshill House, designed by Leonard Vincent as the headquarters of Stevenage Development Corporation, shown shortly after its completion in 1961.
[Stevenage Museum]

Figure 60
The Head Post Office, built in 1958–9 and
demolished in 1999. The premises of Barclays Bank
Ltd are just visible on the left.
[Stevenage Museum]

In order to bolster the economies of the project, retail space was included on the ground floor of Daneshill House. Most of this was leased by Midland Bank, which was responsible for fitting the area out. Originally, it had been intended that these units would lead into a planned pedestrian shopping link between Danestrete and the Great North Road, but this scheme was abandoned in the mid-1960s. The ground floor also included a reception area for the Corporation offices and, at the foot of the main staircase, a large tiled map of the new town, based on the revised Master Plan of 1955. This is believed to date from *c.* 1960 and to be the work of Carter's of Poole (*see* p. 4).

At the Head Post Office, which like Daneshill House overlooked the bus station and the Town Square, the lower two floors were used by Post Office staff while general accommodation was provided on the storeys above (Fig. 60). Initially, these were occupied by the Inland Revenue. A more utilitarian single-storey sorting office was added to the rear in 1961–2, along with a canteen and clubroom which could be enjoyed by all the building's occupants.

Langley House, on the site to the immediate south of the Head Post Office, was begun as a speculative development by the Development Corporation as part of its efforts to attract office employment to the new town. By spring 1960 a deal had been struck with British Railways, who took on the building for their Eastern Region. A team of around 200 people moved into their new premises in October the following year. The building was lower in height than Daneshill House and the Head Post Office, having three main storeys (Fig. 61).

In the 1960s, two further office blocks were built further north on Danestrete: Swingate House and Brickdale House. These both had specific clients, respectively the Lloyds Bank Branches Clearing Centre and the Ministry of Public Building and Works. Swingate House was designed by Vincent's team

Figure 61
Langley House, Southgate, built in 1959–60 and demolished in c. 2003.
[Stevenage Museum]

Figure 62
A photograph of 1967 showing the phase I block of
Brickdale House (built 1964–6), with work beginning
on phase II to the north.
[Stevenage Museum]

and built in 1961–2. Brickdale House – also known at the time as the 'Crown offices' development – was designed by the Ministry's staff in liaison with the Corporation and built in phases. An L-shaped complex was erected in 1964–6 and *c.* 1967–8, and this was extended to the west and south in the 1970s and 1980s. It was intended primarily as offices for the Land Registry, but also catered for government departments including the Inland Revenue and the Ministry of Labour – therefore bringing significant employment opportunities to the centre of Stevenage. The early ranges of Brickdale House were a slightly later form of the model adopted for the Head Post Office and Langley House, with expanses of glazing and coloured panels beneath the windows (Fig. 62). However, Swingate House was taller and more austere, being clad in dark-coloured vitreous glass mosaic (Fig. 63). The top floor included a staff dining room and managers' dining room, with balconies opening south.

The final office block built in Stevenage town centre during this period was on the east side of the town, next to the county buildings. The need for this block became pressing when construction of the town hall and municipal buildings at the north of the town centre was postponed. In September 1962 the Corporation

Figure 63 left top
The south front of Swingate House, built in 1961–2 as offices for the Lloyds Bank Branches Clearing Centre. [DP275643, James O. Davies]

Figure 64 above
Vincent & Gorbing's design drawing of 1963 for the Southgate House office block, St George's Way. [Courtesy of Vincent and Gorbing Ltd and Stevenage Museum]

Figure 65 left bottom
View showing the careful design of Southgate House in relation to the tower of St George's Church, the Town Gardens and High Plash flats on the left. [Stevenage Museum]

offered to build 'almost immediately' offices for the temporary use of Stevenage Urban District Council, while planning of the town centre was reconsidered.[79] This block – named Southgate House – was to be located at the junction of Southgate and St George's Way. Leonard Vincent, recently established in private practice with Ray Gorbing, worked up drawings for the new building and these were agreed in principle in January 1963 (Fig. 64). Construction of the reinforced concrete structure began that spring, and the block was ready for occupation in September 1964. It had 15 storeys in all, totalling 70,000 sq. ft (6,503m²) of office space, and featured under-floor heating, three high-speed lifts and double-glazed windows from the sixth floor upwards. Between 1964 and the early 1980s, the first to fourth levels were occupied by the Council, while other occupants included the firm of Vincent & Gorbing, based on the 13th and 14th floors in 1964–88.

The lower floors of Southgate House were finished last. These were fitted out from 1965 as a Watney Mann public house to designs by the brewery's consultant architect, F. Barnard Reyner (1909–87), and opened in October 1966 as the Long Ship. The Viking-themed premises featured a large first-floor restaurant and a 60ft- (18m) long mosaic of a Viking longboat on the exterior – the work of the artist William Mitchell (1925–2020) (*see* p. 153). Both the mosaic and the building's height – it was the tallest building in Stevenage town centre – ensured that Southgate House was a prominent landmark. It was designed with this in mind and carefully sited, especially in relation to the Town Centre Gardens and the campanile of St George's Church (Fig. 65).

Buildings for entertainment and leisure

As has been noted, the area to the west of the bus station was set aside in the original plans of Stevenage for entertainment buildings, which the town centre sorely lacked in its earliest years. Initially, the Development Corporation hoped to build a cinema here and entered into negotiations in the mid-1950s with ABC and Rank (Odeon). However, these proved fruitless and by 1958 attention had shifted instead to a dance hall.

Design work on the new Stevenage dance hall was undertaken by Vincent's team in collaboration with Mr A. Askew of Mecca. This company had successfully diversified into dance halls in 1927, and by the 1950s was enjoying immense popularity – with most halls taking the name 'Locarno' from the showcase venue in Streatham, South London. By 1961 Mecca operated 41 venues across Britain, with several more planned. Designs for the Stevenage 'Locarno' were produced in 1958, a model of the scheme was completed in 1960 and construction began later that year.

The new dance hall opened in a blaze of publicity in October 1961. Mecca invited 800 guests to the venue's first night, and the large ballroom – designed to hold around 2,000 dancers plus 700 'sitters out' – was full. Guests were promised 'West End entertainment and catering in a real live setting at the Stevenage Locarno'.[80] Externally, the new building was comparatively simple. It had a low brick front range with a projecting canopy, and a taller aluminium-clad ballroom block to the rear (Fig. 66 and *see* p. 152). Internally, however, it was anything but plain. The double-height ballroom, edged on three sides by a balcony, had a revolving stage and a 'night-sky ceiling', thousands of tiny lights 'offering an Arabian Night-like fantasy' (Fig. 67).[81] Other facilities included a licensed club and restaurant, beautifully appointed ladies' 'boudoirs' and gentlemen's 'stag rooms' complete with electric presses and razors for men who went dancing straight from work. Following the legislation of play for stakes

Figure 66
The Mecca dance hall in Danestrete, built in 1960–1.
Daneshill House can be seen on the site to the left.
[Stevenage Museum]

Figure 67
The ballroom of the Mecca dance hall featured a
revolving stage and an elaborate lighting scheme.
This view dates from 1961.
[Stevenage Museum]

under the Betting and Gaming Act of 1960, Mecca also operated bingo halls and changed the Stevenage venue to this use in the 1970s.

Even before the dance hall was complete, plans were in hand for another entertainment facility, to be constructed on the adjacent site in Danestrete. This was the bowling alley, which built upon a new national craze – ten-pin bowling had spread to the United Kingdom from America, with the first commercial bowling hall opening in North London in January 1960. The proposal for the Stevenage venue was announced in August that year, and construction began in autumn 1961. Design was undertaken under Leonard Vincent in liaison with the client firm, Ambassador Bowling Ltd – a subsidiary of Associated Television (ATV) (Fig. 68).

The Stevenage venue was the first bowling centre in any British new town and one of the largest in England at that date. It opened to press and public in August 1962, and an official ceremony was held the following month. The actor Roger Moore, star of the ATV series *The Saint*, inaugurated the centre's lanes by

Figure 68
The Ambassador Lanes bowling centre, built in
Danestrete in 1961–2. The structure was demolished
in c. 2002.
[Stevenage Museum]

rolling the 'Golden Ball'. The bowling centre, open seven days a week, proved immediately popular: the press noted that on 6 October 1962, 1,000 people visited for its Saturday session.[82] Like the front range of the Mecca dance hall, the bowling centre had a low, broad profile, which was simply designed. It was faced in the incised concrete aggregate used elsewhere in the town centre. Within, the emphasis was the bowling lanes – there were 26 in all, with room for 130 players and 150 spectators. The centre also included a Wimpy Bar, part of a chain of snack bars and restaurants which had arrived in Britain in 1954.

Another important leisure facility for Stevenage, opened just a month after the bowling centre, was the swimming pool. This was a Stevenage Council project, intended by at least the early 1950s and allotted to the east side of St George's Way. Designs for the swimming pool were produced by Leonard Vincent and construction was undertaken in 1961–2. On the pool's completion, the Corporation's journal noted that 'It can fairly be said that in a town where something new is almost commonplace, few events have been more eagerly awaited than this', describing the pool as perhaps 'the most valuable recreational asset the town has yet acquired'.[83]

Externally, the swimming baths were striking (Fig. 69). The south-facing windows of the pool hall were formed within a curtain-walled grid similar to that used for the commercial buildings of the town centre. Originally, sliding doors from the pool hall opened onto a sunbathing terrace, overlooking the Town Centre Gardens. Unfortunately, the recladding of the building in 2000–1 has

Figure 69
The swimming pool at the time of its completion in 1962.
The large gridded windows lighting the pool hall were
covered over in c. 2000.
[Stevenage Museum]

Figure 70
The interior of the pool hall in a view of 1963.
[Architectural Press Archive/RIBA Collections]

obscured all trace of this attractive feature. Within, the baths featured a large swimming pool built to competition standards and a smaller training pool, the whole overlooked by a raked spectator gallery (Fig. 70). At the south-west of the building was a 'light and airy' café, directly accessible from the terrace.[84]

The most ambitious of all the 'fringe' buildings of these years was arguably the Bowes Lyon House youth centre. Its construction met a particular need – there was acknowledged to be a disproportionately high number of young people in Stevenage, as in other new towns – and followed on from years of research undertaken both nationally and locally. The design of the building was produced by Leonard Vincent in his new freelance capacity as part of the firm Vincent & Gorbing. In May 1962 the Development Corporation released details of the project, deemed a 'palace for teenagers'.[85] Built for the Stevenage Youth Trust, the centre had an experimental form – a 'revolutionary' reinforced concrete raft was placed 12ft (3.7m) above the ground, carrying the first floor.[86]

Construction began in 1964 and the building opened the following year, named after Sir David Bowes-Lyon (1902–61), Lord Lieutenant of Hertfordshire and former Chairman of the Stevenage Youth Trust (Fig. 71). It was described as 'probably the largest and most important thing of its kind in the country'.[87] Bowes Lyon House was planned flexibly – 'because fashions change rapidly with the young'.[88] Its total floor space of nearly 30,000 sq. ft (2,787m²) allowed for a wide range of functions and activities, including archery, basketball, badminton,

Figure 71
Bowes Lyon House youth centre, built in 1964–5 to designs by Vincent & Gorbing. Original features include the abstract mural on the west and a first-floor 'promenade gallery'.
[DP278930, Patricia Payne]

football, weight training, table tennis, judo, art, theatre, dancing, live music and cinema. An especially innovative feature at the south-west corner of the building was a large space for open-air games, partly open on two sides. Originally, this included a roller-skating rink, but it proved a 'white elephant' and was filled in less than a year after the centre's opening.[89]

On the first floor, the youth centre included two large halls – one generally used for sports and the other for drama and entertainments – plus a coffee bar, which was open to the public. There were views over the Town Centre Gardens, while a 'promenade gallery' or 'sunbathing terrace' ran around the whole upper level. Internal decoration was simple and functional; walls were mostly of brick, left plain or unpainted. The building's exterior was faced on two sides by horizontal panels of precast concrete aggregate – like that used throughout the town centre – and on the main façade there was an abstract mural by P. J. Ellis, signifying the Seven Ages of Man and their interests.

Bowes Lyon House quickly attracted youth from the area. By early 1966, nearly 2,000 young people aged between 14 and 25 paid to use its facilities weekly. At first there was an emphasis on commercial use and various notable musicians performed there, including Paul Simon and David Bowie. However, its plan was not ideally suited to such profit-based activities and in 1967 financial responsibility for the centre passed to Hertfordshire County Council, allowing the building to function 'more clearly in the manner for which it was designed'.[90]

Public amenities

The public buildings of the town centre were designed to serve Stevenage as a whole and in many cases supplemented or replaced existing amenities. For instance, St George's Church succeeded the 600-year-old St Nicholas's as Stevenage's principal church when for a time the town was administered as a single parish. Located on St George's Way, this was the first public building to be initiated in the town centre. It was the work of the diocese of St Albans, which entrusted its design to John Seely (1899–1963), Lord Mottistone, of the firm Seely & Paget.

The foundation stone of the church was laid in July 1956, its site was cleared from March 1959 and by the end of that year its reinforced concrete framework

Figure 72
St George's Church (now St Andrew and St George),
built in 1956–60 to designs by Seely & Paget.
[DP278139, Patricia Payne]

had been completed, with a tall bell tower or campanile at its south-west corner. This was aligned directly with Market Place, creating a focal point in the view eastwards as well as a landmark for the wider area (*see* Fig. 41). Work moved to the interior of the church in early 1960 and the building was formally consecrated that November, in the presence of the Queen Mother. St George's was designed as a structure of striking modern design though with a traditional plan, and at that time was the largest parish church built in England since the Second World War (Fig. 72).

While work on the church was underway, construction had begun on public buildings located in Southgate, to the immediate south of the shopping precinct. This island plot of land had initially been allocated entirely to Hertfordshire County Council, with various schemes drawn up between 1955 and 1958. By the time the layout gained final approval in September 1958, however, various changes had been made. Additions to the programme were a building constructed for the Regional Hospital Board and The Towers, a residential point block designed by Stevenage Development Corporation and built in 1960–3. The Corporation retained ultimate design control throughout, but this range of different clients is reflected in the more varied architecture of Southgate.

Figure 73
The police station in Southgate (built in 1959–60), viewed across the East Gate car park, with The Towers point block (1960–3) on the right.
[DP278929, Patricia Payne]

In the final scheme, the County Council built two buildings – the police station and the conjoined library and health centre. The former was designed in 1958 under the County Architect C. H. Aslin (1893–1959), in liaison with Leonard Vincent. Construction was undertaken in 1959–60 and the building was formally opened in January 1961. It replaced the earlier police station in Stanmore Road, Old Stevenage, and comprised a simply designed three-storey block with a cell block, drill yard, parade room and offices to the rear (Fig. 73). The building's use as a police station was, however, to prove short-lived. By early 1963 it was already found to be too small, and in the mid- to late 1960s a reorganisation of the local police force meant the need for larger premises became urgent. It was replaced by a police station built in 1972–4 on the west side of Lytton Way and was subsequently used as a social services centre.

The other Hertfordshire County Council building on Southgate has proved far more enduring, in terms of fulfilling its original use. This is the county library and county health centre, which form halves of a unified structure designed in

Figure 74
The county library and health centre, built in 1959–60 to designs by the architects of Hertfordshire County Council, with The Towers beyond.
[Stevenage Museum]

Figure 75
The pram shelter at the rear of the health centre: infant welfare clinics were the main function of the building.
[DP275688, James O. Davies]

Figure 76
The interior of the children's lending library on the ground floor of the Southgate building as reworked and extended in 1961–4.
[Stevenage Museum]

1958–9 and built in 1959–60 (Fig. 74 and *see* p. 152). The library was formally opened in January 1961 by the poet Cecil Day-Lewis (1904–72), while the health centre was in use from October 1960 and formally opened in May 1961. The latter's primary function was to provide infant welfare clinics and a notable surviving feature is a covered pram shelter at the rear, originally adjacent to a 'play terrace' (Fig. 75).

By the time of the library's opening, it was already clear that it was inadequate for the needs of Stevenage's rising population. Detailed plans for 'phase II', which increased the library's accommodation from 4,000 sq. ft (372m²) to 12,000 sq. ft (1,115m²), were prepared in early 1960 and work began shortly afterwards. As completed in February 1964, the expanded library included a junior library in the main, front block (Fig. 76), and an adults' library over the two floors at the rear.

On the immediate west of the library is the outpatients' clinic, the final public building on Southgate. This was built for the North-West Metropolitan Regional Hospital Board and administered as an annexe of the Lister Hospital in Hitchin; a dedicated hospital for Stevenage, located at Corey's Mill, was only opened in 1972. For the design, the Hospital Board turned to one of their approved consultant architects, Peter Dunham (1911–97) of the firm Messrs

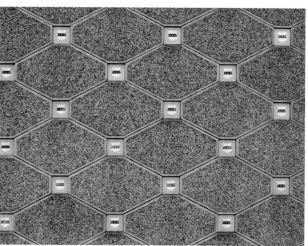

Dunham, Widdup and Harrison. He produced designs in 1958, and the clinic was constructed in 1960–1.

In its general form, Stevenage's outpatients' clinic followed the model of a similar building in Corby new town, designed by John Weeks of Llewelyn Davies and Weeks in 1955. It is made up of blocks of differing sizes, and has a prominent corner range faced in the exposed aggregate panels which were so favoured by Leonard Vincent and the Development Corporation (Fig. 77). Here, the aggregate was used in precast diamond panels with tiles at the intersections, giving it a quilted effect (Fig. 78). Internally, this corner block contained a double-height gymnasium which served the physiotherapy department. Other facilities included a pharmacy and consultation, examination and X-ray rooms. On the west side of the building, a notable survival is the railed staircase and rampway which provided access to the clinic for disabled people and those in wheelchairs. Two existing Scots pines in this area were carefully retained as part of the Corporation's wider landscaping policy.

The third and last structure built by Hertfordshire County Council in the town centre during this period was the fire and ambulance station – originally intended for Southgate, but ultimately constructed on the east side of St George's Way. This was designed by the County Architect's team in 1960 and built in 1961–2 (Fig. 79). Interestingly, the height of its hose drying tower had to be

Figure 77
The outpatients' clinic completed in 1961 for the North-West Metropolitan Regional Hospital Board, to designs by Peter Dunham.
[Stevenage Museum]

Figure 78
The outpatients' clinic features the aggregate facing used elsewhere in the town centre, but here took the form of precast diamond panels set with tiles.
[DP275681, James O. Davies]

Figure 80
The Central Garage, constructed in 1960–1 to designs by Max Lock, included a car showroom and a filling station. The site was redeveloped as flats in 2005–6.
[Stevenage Museum]

reduced at the request of the Development Corporation, 'to ensure no visual conflict' with the campanile of St George's Church, situated to the north.[91]

Although not a public amenity in the formal sense, a further building is worthy of note: the Central Garage, which was conveniently set at the entrance to Danestrete – the vehicular gateway to the heart of the town centre. The complex, which comprised a car showroom, petrol station and garage or motorists' shop, was built by the firm Shell-Mex BP Ltd in 1960–1. At that time, it was the only petrol and service station in Stevenage town centre, and proved 'a boon to many motorists'.[92] For the designs, Shell turned to the respected architect-planner Max Lock (1909–88). He produced a structure of unusual and eye-catching design, with a showroom comprised of a two-storey glass box (Fig. 80).

6

The town centre after 1965 – expansion and change

The proposals for expanding the size and population of Stevenage new town – considered from summer 1962 – continued to have an impact on development in the later 1960s and 1970s. Although the government announced in April 1965 that the town would not expand to a target of 150,000, no firm decision was taken about what the ultimate population would be. This led to an air of uncertainty, and Stevenage Development Corporation had no choice but to plan for the likelihood of rising numbers of residents and visitors to the town centre. In 1966 Leonard Vincent produced a new Master Plan; approved the following year, this controlled development in Stevenage throughout the remaining years of the Corporation's life and allowed for an ultimate population of 105,000.

In order to cater for higher population figures, changes were needed – including to the road network, educational facilities and town centre provision. A plan prepared by Vincent in September 1967 included additional shops at the north of Queensway, a U-shaped civic centre complex at the north-west and a number of new facilities on the west fringe of the town centre, including a railway station, skating rink, cinema and arts centre. It also proposed two new dual carriageways bounding the town centre: Fairlands Way ('Road 5') on the north and Lytton Way ('Road 10') on the west. Not all of these proposals went ahead, but some did. For instance, both Fairlands Way and Lytton Way were completed in 1969–70 and shortly after this St George's Way – on the east of the town centre – was rebuilt as a dual carriageway (Fig. 81).

One of the aspects of the proposals that did not go ahead was the civic centre. Stevenage Urban District Council remained desperate for its own dedicated offices – by the late 1960s it had occupied for around five years accommodation at Southgate House that had been intended as temporary. For its part, the Development Corporation emphasised that a site should be found which 'would be a credit to the Council and the Town', and in 1974 Leonard Vincent produced details of a scheme at the north-west corner of the town centre.[93] However, although negotiations continued until March 1976, space was tight and land was increasingly valuable to the Corporation. Moreover, by that time, it had become clear that the Corporation would soon be wound up, leaving its offices at Daneshill House and Swingate House vacant. The Council – redubbed Stevenage Borough Council following the local government reorganisation of 1974 – moved into these following the dissolution of the Corporation in 1980, marking an end to decades of plans for a dedicated

Aerial photograph of Stevenage town centre in 1986, looking north-west.
[Stevenage Museum]

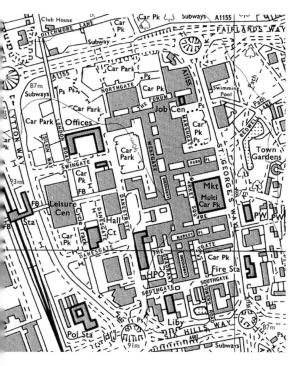

Figure 81
Ordnance Survey map of 1987 showing features including Stevenage town centre's expanded road network, enlarged shopping precinct and railway station.

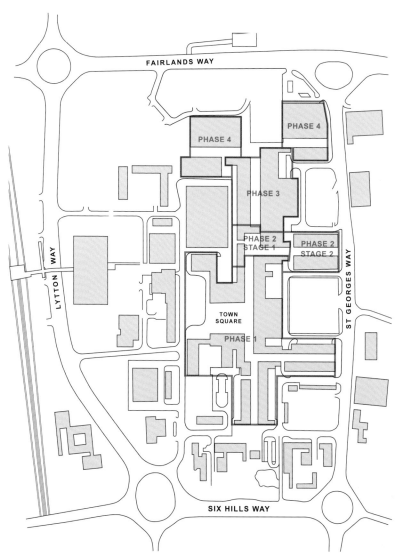

Figure 82
Phased plan of the shopping precinct, based on a drawing published by Stevenage Borough Council in 1981. The dates of building construction are: phase I (1956–9); phase II (1962–4); phase III (1967–70); phase IV (1970–6).

municipal complex. Stevenage town centre is reduced in scale and grandeur by the absence of a major civic building – though Daneshill House was later altered to provide a civic suite.

The late 1960s and 1970s saw the increasing involvement of commissioned architects. Due to a change in official policy, the Development Corporation had reluctantly to pass building work to private developers, and the range of architects working on Stevenage town centre broadened from this time. David Rixson of Vincent & Gorbing, unofficial deputy to Leonard Vincent in his consultancy work to the Development Corporation, has commented that these external agencies produced an architecture that was 'less disciplined'.[94] However, the involvement of Vincent, Gorbing and their former colleagues at the Corporation was vital in ensuring continuity.

Extension of the shopping precinct, 1967–76

Site works for 'phase III' of the shopping precinct were finally begun in 1967, once the Master Plan of 1966 had been approved. Initially, work focused on the top of Queensway, north of the two-storey bridge constructed in 1962–3 (Fig. 82). Detailed plans for the blocks in this area had been completed in 1961, under Leonard Vincent (*see* p. 64). These were dusted off and put to use, the programme of work involving the construction of two parallel ranges.

As planned in 1961, there were 14 shop premises on the west side and eight on the east; the latter were far larger in scale than most of the shops built thus far, and backed onto their own yards. Both blocks had further commercial space on their first- and second-floor levels and there were additional retail units on the north returns, forming the start of the new Forum pedestrian way. External design followed the ethos of the earlier work in the precinct, the blocks being of three storeys with projecting first-floor canopies above the shop windows. There were also cross canopies traversing this part of Queensway, following the approach taken in previous decades (Fig. 83). However, the design was updated for the times: the panels beneath the upper windows of the shopping parades were clad in slate, and strong vertical elements were incorporated between the glazing, faced with concrete aggregate, rising upwards in places to form a parapet.

Figure 83
A photograph of north Queensway, built in 1967–70. The original cross canopies were removed around 1990.
[Stevenage Museum]

Figure 84
This block in The Forum, built in 1971–3, contained a Tesco supermarket and a cinema. The original cross canopies are also visible. The building was demolished in c. 1995.
[Stevenage Museum]

The extended area of Queensway featured various national retailers, drawn to Stevenage by the rising population figures and the continued success of the shopping precinct. In the east block, these included Sainsbury's (at nos 89–91), which moved here from smaller premises by the Town Square. Opened on 7 October 1969, the new store was briefly the largest Sainsbury's trading in the country, with a sales area of 13,800 sq. ft (1,282m²). In the same block, at 85 Queensway, was a large Marks & Spencer store, opened in April 1970. Other new arrivals of this time were Mothercare and Timothy Whites, while the Littlewoods store to the south was extended.

In late 1969, as 'phase III' was approaching completion, site work started to the immediate north, along The Forum. It was from this point that the Development Corporation made use of external architects, rather than designing buildings themselves. However, although the style of the buildings naturally diversified to some degree, both Leonard Vincent and the Corporation's Chief

Figure 85
Advert for the Grampian Hotel in The Forum, opened
in 1973.
[Stevenage Museum]

Architect Leslie Aked – who was succeeded in 1979 by his own deputy, Brian
Alford – kept a tight hold on the process, helping to promote and maintain the
town centre 'concept'.

One of the first components of 'phase IV' of the shopping precinct was the
large commercial block built at the north-east corner of the town centre, to
designs by the architects Inskip & Witzynski. This was constructed in 1971–3
and included a Tesco supermarket and an ABC cinema (Fig. 84). The latter,
seating a total of 600 people, was a major new facility for Stevenage; it came
shortly after discussions had broken down with Rank regarding a site to the rear
of Daneshill House. The land opposite the ABC was developed with a similar
commercial block in *c.* 1976.

In the west part of The Forum, beyond Queensway, work on a retail and
hotel scheme was begun in 1970. At the lower level it included nine shops and
above this rose the seven-storey, brick-faced Grampian Hotel. The hotel was the
work of Hatfield-based architectural firm Archer Boxer Partners and was
completed in early 1973 (Fig. 85). It was considered a luxury amenity at the
time, built for 'discerning visitors to Stevenage'.[95] The hotel boasted 100
bedrooms – all with a private bathroom, television and telephone – while the
first floor included the hotel reception, a cocktail bar, grill room and 350-person
banqueting suite.

Opposite, on the north side of The Forum, a branch of C&A was completed in 1975 (Fig. 86). This was the work of the Manchester-based architects Leach, Rhodes & Walker, who designed a number of C&A stores. It was a blocky structure built with a concrete frame faced in exposed aggregate panels. Adjacent to this, in 1976, a branch of British Home Stores was opened (Fig. 87). The incised lines in the aggregate of both buildings continued the design theme set by the first-phase works of the 1950s. Another element ensuring continuity and unity of the shopping precinct as a whole was the cross canopies. These ran north–south across The Forum – in both parts, either side of Queensway – joining the 1970s buildings together (see Fig. 84).

Naturally, the extension of the shopping precinct brought with it a need for increased parking. Leonard Vincent's revised town centre layout of 1967 proposed seven multistorey car parks, including three on St George's Way, on the sites of surface car parks. This idea was not new. By 1963, with Stevenage's car parks already full at peak periods, the Development Corporation was considering multistorey schemes, and the town's surface car parks had been designed to allow 'decking over should the need arise', with a total capacity of 12,000 cars.[96]

However, in the end, only one multistorey car park was built during the Corporation's lifetime, largely due to financial restrictions and a government moratorium on the construction of such buildings during the 1970s. The one that went ahead occupied the site of the Market Square car park. Initial plans were produced in 1963, but the height of the proposed structure proved controversial and it was only in 1968–9 that revised designs were produced and approved. The building had parking on three main storeys above ground, plus

Figure 86
View of 1998 showing the C&A in The Forum, with the BHS beyond. These stores were opened in 1975 and 1976 respectively.
[Courtesy of K. Morrison]

Figure 87
The BHS in The Forum viewed from the south-west in 2020. The store closed in 2016.
[DP275715, James O. Davies]

Figure 88
The multistorey car park on St George's Way, built in
1971–3 on the site of the former Market Square car
park.
[DP275700, James O. Davies]

Figure 89
The indoor market at the time of its opening in
December 1973.
[Stevenage Museum]

Figure 90
One of the underpasses created beneath St George's
Way in 1971–3. It was decorated with relief sculptures
by the artist William Mitchell.
[DP278118, Patricia Payne]

further space on the roof and at basement level. It was constructed using a Bison precast concrete framework in 1971–3, with space at the rear of the ground floor for an indoor market – on the same site on which the open market had been held since 1959 (Figs 88 and 89).

Alongside the construction of the multistorey car park, St George's Way was rebuilt as a dual carriageway. This was not without its complexities: work involved the raising of the road slightly and some tricky engineering due to the culvert for the Stevenage brook. However, the desired result was achieved: the new car park connected directly to both sides of St George's Way through the creation of a vehicular underpass. Pedestrian underpasses were also created, linking the shopping precinct with Town Centre Gardens and the area beyond. These feature relief sculptures of 1973 by the artist William Mitchell (Fig. 90).

The new town railway station and the elevated walkway

Plans for a dedicated railway station for Stevenage new town had first been sketched out in the mid-1940s. A site was agreed in 1946, but – given the existence of the Victorian station in Old Stevenage – construction was not a major priority. British Railways noted in 1953 that they only expected to build a new station 'when the condition of the traffic justifies it' and when the old station had been outgrown.[97] In 1961 the project was under discussion again but it fell foul of railway cuts and the delayed programme of work at Stevenage.

Finally, in 1966, initial designs for the station were produced in liaison with Vincent & Gorbing. Detailed designs followed in 1971; these were the work of Harold Ormiston, Chief Civil Engineer for British Rail's Eastern Region, and BR's Regional Architect, Sydney Hardy. Widening of the railway track was begun in summer 1971, and the new station was opened for trains in July 1973 – a day after the closure of the station at Old Stevenage (Fig. 91). This was a major landmark in the new town's history, and helped to make Stevenage easily accessible to a broader population.

As had been intended by Stevenage Development Corporation since at least 1961, the new station was linked to the new town centre by a pedestrian walkway. The design of this was entrusted to R. B. (Roy) Lenthall (1924–2008),

Figure 91
The railway station on the west of the new town centre was built in 1971–3 to replace the Victorian station at Old Stevenage.
[DP275655, James O. Davies]

Figure 92
View looking west from Danestrete, showing the early
1970s pedestrian walkway linking the town centre
with the railway station.
[DP278094, Patricia Payne]

Figure 93
The underside of the early 1970s concrete walkway, at
its junction with the arts and leisure centre.
[DP275653, James O. Davies]

Chief Engineer at the Corporation, and undertaken in 1971. The first section was completed at the same time as the railway station, in the second half of 1973. This was raised 18ft (5.5m) above Lytton Way and was subsequently extended to pass through the upper level of the arts and leisure centre. The walkway was fully opened in 1975, and sloped gently down from the arts and leisure centre towards Danestrete (Figs 92 and 93). In order to ensure that the walkway was of sufficient size and status, the Corporation arranged for the removal of a mature tree and the rebuilding of the north side of the Mecca dance hall. The result remains an effective, practical and attractive element of Stevenage's townscape, and one of its most powerful pieces of planning.

The arts and leisure centre

The confirmed plans for a railway station focused greater attention and interest on the west part of Stevenage town centre. Leonard Vincent's layout plan of 1967 showed a cluster of buildings proposed for this area, but only a few were actually constructed – by far the most significant being the arts and leisure centre, the last major project undertaken by the Development Corporation.

This initiative originated in the early 1960s, when the need for a permanent arts centre was highlighted by local groups including the Stevenage Arts Guild.

Initial plans by Vincent & Gorbing were unveiled in autumn 1965, and a site was identified to the west of the old Great North Road. Meanwhile, that same year a separate trust began to explore the possibility of an indoor sports centre for Stevenage. This was inspired by the one opened in Harlow new town a year earlier. In January 1968 the Eastern Sports Council suggested that the two interests work together to plan a single, shared building – then a novel concept. The designs, produced by Raymond Gorbing of Vincent & Gorbing, were given initial approval in 1971, and the foundation stone was laid in June 1974. By November 1975 Stevenage's new centre was in use and it was formally opened in February 1976, being described in the architectural press as 'among the most fully developed and wide-ranging leisure centres in Britain'.[98]

The centre was designed as a building of two main parts. On the south were the sports facilities and on the north were facilities for the arts, though this division was not strictly adhered to. There were three main spaces, dominating the building's plan and rising through all three levels: a sports hall to the south-east; a bowls hall to the north-east (Fig. 94); and a 507-seat theatre to the north-west. The latter was named after the influential actor and theatre director Edward Gordon Craig (1872–1966), born in Stevenage to the actress Ellen Terry. Access to the centre was originally via a second-floor entrance, reached via the elevated walkway which passed through the building.

Figure 94
A photograph of 2017 showing the bowls hall within the arts and leisure centre, built in 1974–5 to designs by Raymond Gorbing.
[DP236998, Patricia Payne]

Figure 95
The west side of the arts and leisure centre in a photograph of 1988, prior to remodelling. The building's cladding led it to be known locally as 'Gorbing's Orange Box'.
[Stevenage Museum]

The external design proved somewhat controversial. Built of reinforced concrete, the centre was faced almost entirely in panels of reinforced orange-coloured fibreglass (GRP). These were arranged as rectangles and gave the building a padded effect, while their colour led the building to be known locally as 'Gorbing's Orange Box' (Fig. 95 and *see* p. 92). GRP breaks down on exposure to sunlight and the panels did not last long; in the early 1990s the entire building was reclad.

The dissolution of Stevenage Development Corporation

Under the provisions of the New Towns Act of 1946, new town development corporations were intended to be temporary, the government being given the power to 'wind up' these bodies when they had completed their work. A second New Towns Act in 1959 established a Commission for the New Towns, a national body which was to take over and manage new town property when each settlement was completed. The Commission was set up in 1961 and by 1979 owned assets in four of Britain's new towns, its focus being industrial and commercial buildings.[99] As other towns approached completion, the New Towns (Amendment) Act of 1976 enabled the transfer of other new town assets, such as housing, shops and public houses, to local authorities.

In 1977, the Labour government announced that the development corporations of Stevenage and many other first-phase new towns, including Harlow, Bracknell and Basildon, would be wound up in the next five years. This moment had always been anticipated, but it was accelerated due to increased criticism of the new towns programme and greater emphasis on the regeneration of inner cities. From this point on, the clock was ticking for Stevenage Development Corporation and it began to draw its various programmes of work to a close.

On 1 April 1978 and 1 April 1980, the Corporation handed all the property it could to Stevenage Borough Council, including around 150 shops. The Council attempted, through the Stevenage Development Authority Bill (1979–80), to gain control of further buildings, but this was defeated by government and on 1 July 1980 industrial, commercial and other assets in the town were formally

Figure 96
Plaque on the clock tower in the Town Square, added following the dissolution of Stevenage Development Corporation in 1980.
[DP233332, Derek Kendall]

1946-1980

During these years the Stevenage Development Corporation was responsible for planning and building the New Town of Stevenage

vested in the Commission for the New Towns. The remainder of the Corporation's assets were sold on the open market at great speed, in spite of protests, at the behest of a new Conservative government hostile to public corporations. Later, as a result of the same government pressure for the realisation of new town assets, the Commission was forced to dispose of many of the freeholds. In 1981 a Stevenage Borough Council report noted that 'It is likely that the major part of the shopping area will pass into private ownership during the next few years' – a change which had significant consequences for Stevenage town centre's appearance and unity.[100]

On 30 September 1980, Stevenage Development Corporation was formally dissolved and control of the town passed to Stevenage Borough Council (Fig. 96). Thus ended what had been a somewhat fraught relationship between two separate authorities but a vital period of vision, energy and productivity on the part of both. The Development Corporation had done an admirable job of creating a strong and enduring concept for the town centre and Stevenage as a whole, following that through with building work and then maintaining the town with the same ideals.

Stevenage was luckier than many other new towns. It was complete by the time of the Corporation's dissolution, and Stevenage Borough Council had been so long and closely involved with the Corporation's work that it had a very good understanding of the approach that should be taken. However, without owning all the relevant freeholds, it was difficult to enforce a unifying 'concept' in the way that had been imposed by the Corporation.

Construction work of the 1980s

In the first decade after the dissolution of Stevenage Development Corporation, comparatively few changes were made to the town centre. In part, this reflected an increasing focus on retail parks and edge-of-town facilities. The Roaring Meg retail park, for instance, was built in 1987–8 to the south of the town centre. There were, however, two major schemes undertaken during these years, both constructed in 1987–8. The first was the Westgate shopping centre, designed in 1986 by the firm Renton Howard Wood Levin. The need for this 'specialist shopping provision' – which comprised an enclosed mall with central atrium

Figure 97
The Tesco superstore, built in 1987–8 to designs by Vincent, Gorbing & Partners.
[DP278149, Patricia Payne]

Figure 98
Daneshill House from the south-east, showing the extensions undertaken by Stevenage Borough Council in c. 1985–6.
[DP278097, Patricia Payne]

and multistorey car parking above – had been highlighted in 1983–4 by the Council; it formed part of the 'continued development of the town as a major sub-regional shopping centre'.[101] The second was the Tesco superstore, built to designs prepared in 1985–6 by the firm Vincent, Gorbing & Partners (Fig. 97). Both of these developments were inserted into the existing townscape in a way that did not detract from the earlier buildings. The Westgate Centre was built in a discrete position to the rear of Queensway and The Forum, on the site of the former Westgate surface car park, while the Tesco complex was built on a fresh site at the north-west corner of the town centre.

In terms of existing buildings, the most notable alterations were those made by Stevenage Borough Council to Daneshill House, which it inherited from the Corporation in 1980. For the first time since the start of the new town, the Council was able to occupy its own dedicated office space, and it initiated a programme of remodelling to adapt the building to its new use. By 1985 the area around Daneshill House was a building site; its exterior was reclad the following year, and a new two-storey entrance range was built by the Mecca dance hall, projecting forwards over the pavement. Within the building, the Council created a council chamber and civic suite. To house these new facilities and associated civic space, Daneshill House was substantially extended to the rear (Fig. 98).

Other changes in this decade were more minor, including the reworking of the bus station in the early to mid-1980s and the removal of two of the

Figure 99
To date, the main alteration to the north part of Queensway has been the replacement of the west and cross canopies with a glazed arcade in c. 1990.
[DP278101, Patrica Payne]

Figure 100
The junction of Queensway and Market Place in 2021. Cross canopies were removed in this area as part of works undertaken in 2005–6.
[DP233287, Derek Kendall]

Figure 101
The south end of Queensway as it appears today, following public realm works. Compare Fig. 46.
[DP278922, Patricia Payne]

Figure 102
Photograph of 1993 showing the completed alterations to the east side of the platform in the Town Square.
[Stevenage Museum]

cross canopies in the central part of Queensway (by Fine Fare and to the immediate north). In 1988 the part of the shopping precinct built in 1956–9 was designated as a conservation area, reflecting growing appreciation of the town centre's architecture. This helped to protect the core area from any substantial change, though the L-shaped block at the north-west of the Town Square was excluded from the conservation area's boundaries.

Construction and changes of the 1990s and early 2000s

The years around the turn of the 21st century proved to be a time of far greater change for Stevenage town centre than the 1980s. Edge-of-town developments like the Stevenage Leisure Park, opened in 1996 on the west of Stevenage station, undoubtedly exacerbated a process of decline, which the town has in common with high streets nationally. In the late 1990s and early 2000s, various businesses left the shopping precinct for the first time since the 1950s and 1960s – often as part of closures or sales of chain stores nationally. For example, the Co-operative store in the Town Square was closed in 1999, the C&A in The Forum ceased trading in 2000, the Littlewoods closed in c. 2002, the Edward the Confessor pub shut its doors in 2006, Woolworth's in Queensway closed in 2008, Marks & Spencer closed in 2015 and the BHS in The Forum shut in 2016.

Throughout this period, the streetscape of the town centre was renewed and altered. Various cross canopies, dating from the late 1950s to the mid-1970s, were removed entirely. For instance, those in the north part of Queensway were taken down around 1990 along with the west block's ground-floor canopies, to be replaced by a glass-roofed walkway (Fig. 99). The 1970s cross canopies of The Forum seem to have been demolished at the same time. Slightly later, as part of public realm works of 2005–6, the cross canopies were removed in the south and central sections of Queensway, changing the character of the area fairly significantly (Figs 100 and 101).

In the Town Square, changes were undertaken to the elevated platform and public toilet block of 1958. This work was carried out in 1992–3 and involved the removal of the original east staircase, the extension of the platform on its east side, the building of two new staircases on a north–south alignment, the replacement of the platform's railings and a slight move of the sculpture *Joy Ride*, with alteration to the plinth (Fig. 102 and *see* Fig. 127). Undertaken to provide additional space for the toilet block, these changes made a dramatic difference to the platform when seen from the east – though the west, north and south sides were left largely untouched. Slightly later, in about 1995, the pool of the clock tower was altered. Its edges were increased in height, the fountain was replaced and tiling in bright primary colours was installed (Fig. 103). In contrast to the platform, the changes to the pool were generally sympathetic to the character and materials of the 1950s work.

It was during the same decade that the first major demolitions occurred in Stevenage town centre. First, in 1993, the bus garage in Danestrete was taken down and replaced in 1994–5 by a single-storey retail development set back from the road, later occupied by Matalan. Then in about 1995 the 1970s commercial block at the north-east of The Forum – built to house Tesco and the ABC cinema – was demolished. This area was redeveloped as a car park for the new Forum Centre, a shopping mall built in 1996–7 to designs by Jeff Downes of the firm Corstophine & Wright Kenzie Lovell Ltd (Fig. 104). In form and materials, this structure is very different to the earlier buildings of the town centre. It occupies a position at the top of Queensway – the site which was once to be developed as a focal point for the new town, the civic centre and municipal complex. In this context, the resulting development can only be viewed with a sense of regret.

In 1999 one of the key components of the first-phase town centre scheme was demolished – the Head Post Office at the corner of the Town Square and Danestrete. This was perhaps the most dramatic intervention to date, since the building had been a fundamental part of Leonard Vincent's vision for the Town Square area. The building was replaced by The Plaza, a substantial licensed premises and leisure development built in 1999–2000 (Fig. 105). As early as the year 2010, this building was being criticised by the Council itself for ignoring the principles 'which underpin the vision of the town centre'.[102]

In the first decade of the 21st century, there was further change in the Danestrete area. In 2002 approval was granted for the demolition of the former Ambassador Lanes bowling centre – in use by Quasar amusements since the 1990s – and the creation on the site of a surface car park. Slightly further south, Langley House – to the rear of the Head Post Office site – was demolished in

Figure 103
Detail showing Franta Belsky's plaque to Lewis Silkin, added on the clock tower's west face in 1974, and the mid-1990s alterations to the pool.
[DP275713, James O. Davies]

2003 and replaced by a Holiday Inn hotel. Then in 2005 permission was granted for the demolition of the Central Garage on the other side of Danestrete and its replacement with a housing development. Elsewhere in the town centre, other more minor but notable changes were undertaken. These included the recladding of the swimming pool building in 2000–1 and the radical remodelling of Manulife House as a hotel, opened in 2009.

Figure 104
The Forum Centre (built 1996–7) viewed from the north-east.
[DP278903, Patricia Payne]

Figure 105
The Plaza, a retail and leisure development built in 1999–2000 on the site of the Head Post Office.
[DP233351, Derek Kendall]

7 Success and impact

The significance and influence of Stevenage town centre

Even before its official opening in April 1959, Stevenage town centre had proved popular and a major draw for shoppers from a wide area.[103] Retailers reported that the Christmas trade of 1959 was 'absolutely astounding', with shoppers having to 'almost fight their way through the crowds' in the precinct.[104] By 1964, a survey was able to show that 50 per cent of shoppers travelled to the town centre by car, some from up to a hundred miles away.[105]

Certainly, Stevenage Development Corporation was thrilled with its creation, and its Chief Architect Leonard Vincent authored a series of articles in major journals highlighting what had been achieved. In particular, given the scale and strength of opposition to the pedestrian scheme in the early 1950s, the Corporation's staff found contentment in the town centre's commercial success. It was noted in 1958 that 'traders have overcome any qualms they may have had over the trading prospects of a pedestrian shopping centre. The rents obtained show that a pedestrian precinct does not adversely affect values'.[106]

Numerous people who had been critical of the scheme, including retailers, politicians and indeed Corporation staff, found they had to eat their words. Jack Balchin, a later General Manager of the Corporation, noted that 'Some Board members, some Council members, the vocal public, not to say the architects who continuously advocated the pedestrian experiment were shown triumphantly right'.[107]

Architects, planners and government officials flocked from around the world to see Stevenage in person, and especially its shopping precinct. In 1958 the Development Corporation noted that visitors regarded Stevenage 'as something of a "wonderland"'.[108] There was a strong sense of pride that, even in its unfinished state, the town centre had 'captured the imagination and fired the enthusiasm of a wide circle of planners and architects, professional organizations, and members and officers of local authorities and national governments from far and near'.[109]

Some of these visitors were British politicians, such as Prime Minister Harold Macmillan, who visited Stevenage in August 1959 and described the town centre as 'one of the best in the country – indeed in the whole world'.[110] Around the same time, a group of MPs and a Ministry of Transport official

Stevenage Town Square in 1958, showing the popularity of the precinct even before its formal opening in April 1959.
[RIBA Collections]

visited the town centre 'to inspect the lay-out of the pedestrian ways' (Fig. 106).[111] The following year, when visiting Stevenage to mark a start on the new A1 bypass, the Minister of Transport Ernest Marples took time to view the town centre, 'particularly from the pedestrian and vehicular traffic separation aspect'.[112] Some visitors were keen to see Stevenage in order to inform projects of their own. For instance, in 1961 representatives of the LCC's 'out county' expanded towns programme visited Stevenage, and two years later the Minister of Health and Local Government in Northern Ireland visited as part of outline planning for the new city of Craigavon in County Armagh.[113]

Visitors from abroad who came to Stevenage at this time included the German Minister of Housing Herr Paul Lücke, who arrived in April 1960, describing the new town as 'An example to everybody', and 35 Dutchmen from the mining town of Geleen, who visited in 1960 as part of research for a planned shopping centre.[114] Over the course of 1962, visitors to Stevenage from other parts of the country and especially from overseas topped the 4,000 mark –

Figure 106
Stevenage attracted numerous visitors, including officials from the Ministry of Transport – shown here looking along Queensway towards the Town Square.
[Stevenage Pictorial, 8 May 1959]

Figure 107
Stevenage Development Corporation was active in promoting the new town, issuing films, articles and books including this publication of 1954.

among them architects from France, Israel, Japan, Sweden and Russia – while in 1963 Stevenage welcomed visitors from some 80 countries.[115] Even in the mid-1970s, Stevenage was still attracting hordes – in 1974–5, 8,145 visitors arrived from 80 different countries.[116] The new town's influence, therefore, spread very wide indeed.

Stevenage Development Corporation, for its part, was active on the international stage – for example, contributing to planning exhibitions held at Ingelheim, Berlin and Geneva in 1961–2.[117] The Corporation initiated a successful programme of promotion for what had been achieved at Stevenage new town as a whole, publishing books and articles and making films whenever possible (Fig. 107). It was probably due to the Corporation's efforts as well as its innovation that the town centre was frequently used as an example in relevant publications – for instance, one of Leonard Vincent's town centre models was illustrated in Wilfred Burns's study *British Shopping Centres: New Trends in Layout and Distribution* (1959), along with models of

Coventry.[118] This process of promotion was still underway in the 1970s, Corporation material drawing attention to Stevenage's many facilities and features, including the precinct.[119]

Two aspects of the town centre attracted particular praise in these early years: the pedestrian nature and innovation of the shopping precinct, and the quality of its architecture and planning. In 1960 the architectural journal *The Builder* spoke of Stevenage as proving 'the undoubted success of an all-pedestrian centre and shopping precinct', due not only to its 'relaxed and convivial atmosphere' but to the fact that the car had been properly catered for, with car parking on the centre's perimeters being welcome and popular.[120] The Development Corporation's Chief Engineer, George Hardy, emphasised the safety this approach provided to all pedestrians, especially children: 'No more do you see harassed mothers clutching at little Johnny or Mary to prevent them running into the road'. Instead, the town centre was full of 'swarms of children running all over the place in perfect safety'.[121]

The pioneering nature of the precinct was widely acknowledged. In 1956 the *Architects' Journal* stated that Stevenage was 'the first pedestrian centre of its size in Europe', while in 1958 *The Surveyor* wrote of it as 'a unique experiment in modern commercial development'.[122] In the following year, Leonard Vincent stated proudly that

> Stevenage Town Centre achieves for the first time complete segregation of pedestrians from traffic. Gloomy prognostications regarding the modern approach are entirely refuted at Stevenage. People have clearly demonstrated that they are prepared to travel considerable distances in order to shop in an area clear of traffic hazards and with ample parking facilities.[123]

In 1985 Gordon Stephenson – one of the early planners of Stevenage – wrote, 'If we do not count Venice, Stevenage was probably the first town in the world to be designed with a pedestrian core'.[124] It was this novelty that made the Stevenage scheme so controversial at the time and attracted such a high degree of interest, especially among those involved in architecture and planning.

Architectural quality and unity

Stevenage town centre is especially notable for its scale and its status as a unified concept. It was built 'of a piece' on virgin ground, with 1960s to 1970s expansion in matching style. While the concept of the development emerged from the minds of various figures, the unifying presence was Leonard Vincent, with his deputy and later partner Raymond Gorbing. As an architect with Stevenage Development Corporation from 1949 and its consultant from 1962 to 1980, Vincent oversaw the design and construction of almost every aspect of the town centre's architecture and layout. Only Frederick Gibberd enjoyed an oversight of a new town comparable to Vincent's, serving as Harlow's consultant architect-planner from 1947 to 1980 – though important shops at the core of his plan, Broad Walk, were built by commercial developers using their own architects.

Where Vincent's team did not produce the designs themselves – as for instance with the buildings erected by Hertfordshire County Council – they provided clear advice to others, and the Corporation had the final say on approved designs. The resulting unity has been discussed in Chapter 4. Stevenage came to be seen as the ideal example of a neat, organised town centre development, a writer of 1958 commenting, 'This is the sort of town that a tidy child might construct with his Meccano set' (Figs 108 and 109).[125]

Figure 108
Market Place in a photograph of 1960, looking north-west towards Queensway.
[Stevenage Museum]

Figure 109
The same view in 2020. Apart from public realm works completed in 2018, the streetscape is largely unchanged.
[DP275698, James O. Davies]

The quality of the work at Stevenage town centre was much commented upon by contemporaries, and it is notable that this level of success was achieved by Vincent and his team despite the considerable constraints on public funding. Stevenage was seen to hold up well against comparable developments: for instance, for Kenneth Robinson, writing in 1962, Stevenage was 'more elegant in its scale and proportion than most of the shopping areas at Coventry'.[126] Jack Balchin wrote in 1980 that Stevenage town centre 'deserves its reputation as not only the earliest of modern pedestrian centres but as one of the best'.[127] In its modernity, it realised suggestions made during the early 1950s by the architectural press, which was critical of more traditionally designed work in other city centres. In particular, the town centre is notable as an early example of curtain walling in Britain, while its neutral framework as a basis for advertising earned it a special feature in the *Architectural Review* in 1957.[128]

For his work on the town centre, Leonard Vincent was appointed a Commander of the Order of the British Empire (CBE) in the New Year's Honours' List of 1960. This was a unique distinction for an architect at a time when those in public offices received little recognition from within the profession. During 1960 Vincent also had the rare accolade of seeing his designs for Stevenage included in the Royal Academy summer exhibition, and was awarded a distinction in town planning by the RIBA; the citation described the town centre as 'a distinguished design ... with all the interest, variety and charm of the traditional English town centre'. The award endorsed 'the generally accepted view that Stevenage centre is one of the most successful in Europe'.[129]

A clear 'concept' covering the layout and design of Stevenage town centre was in place by at least 1949, and this became stronger and more detailed over the subsequent years – especially 1954–66 – in the hands of Leonard Vincent, Ray Gorbing and the architectural staff at the Development Corporation. This unifying concept encompassed the design of details (such as lettering) but also layout, points of visual interest (such as sculpture), boundaries of sites, and the massing and height of buildings. In particular, Vincent realised his idea that the core of the town centre should be limited to three storeys, with taller buildings adding 'architectural interest' at key sites on the perimeters.[130]

The concept was something that bound the work of the 1950s to the expansion phases of the 1960s and 1970s. So it is that features such as the

single-storey cross canopies, concrete aggregate facing and below-canopy hanging signs are as characteristic of the 1956–9 commercial core as of the extensions to the precinct undertaken up to the mid-1970s (Fig. 110). In a note of 1968 Vincent emphasised the importance of this internationally recognised concept, and felt that the integrity of the town centre's design should be protected at all costs.[131] Certainly, it is this concept, and the integrity and unity of design, that is one of the major aspects that makes Stevenage town centre so special – today as in the 1950s. It also makes it unique among British developments of its type, with other new towns having centres of mixed type, date and design.

Figure 110
The use of hanging signs was part of the 'advertisement' scheme formulated for the town centre in 1957. These surviving examples are in The Forum, constructed in the early 1970s.
[DP275709, James O. Davies]

Stevenage's influence on later pedestrian schemes

It is difficult today – when pedestrian planning is the norm for urban centres – to fully appreciate the novelty and pioneering nature of Stevenage town centre. As has been discussed in Chapter 3, very few pedestrian developments were built internationally before the early 1950s. It was for this reason that Stevenage Development Corporation made a particular study of American precincts and the work at Coventry (including the Upper Precinct, built 1954–6), the Lijnbaan in Rotterdam (1951–3) and Vällingby in Sweden (1952–4). However, none of these represented an entirely new town centre development and none were on the same scale as Stevenage. It is telling that in 1951 a representative of the Ministry of Housing and Local Government wrote in relation to the work at Stevenage, 'we have no experience of building a new town centre in this country from scratch'.[132]

As has been shown, the planning process at Stevenage was prolonged and fraught with challenges – the pedestrian scheme had reached a detailed stage by 1950, but was initially opposed and briefly set aside in favour of a vehicular approach in 1953. So it was that the first phase of work on Stevenage town centre – begun in earnest in autumn 1956 – was initiated slightly later in date than the Upper Precinct in Coventry and Harlow Market Square (1955–6), though not fully pedestrianised at that time).

However, Stevenage's town centre was still completed earlier than the vast majority of other British and international comparators. By the end of the 1950s, it had played a major part in showing that pedestrian planning was an option that was financially viable, safer and attractive to the public. From being seen as risky and experimental at the start of that decade, pedestrianisation soon became an accepted approach to town planning. In his 1959 book, Wilfred Burns stated that

> Pedestrian precincts for shoppers, with roads circling the shopping area ... give ideal conditions for shoppers and for the moving vehicle ... It is, in fact, the only sensible plan on which to base designs for shopping centres in the future, whether they be town centres or major suburban centres.[133]

The design of Stevenage town centre found its way into pedestrian precincts large and small, especially those constructed in the 1960s and 1970s. A notable example is the open-air pedestrian precinct at Jarrow, Tyne & Wear, which comprised 93 shops in a T-shaped concourse. This was built by Sam Chippindale, perhaps the most famous developer of shopping precincts, operating as the Arndale Property Trust Ltd with Arnold Hagenbach. The first phase was constructed in 1959–61 to designs by Alan Sunderland and was the earliest Arndale Centre (Fig. 111). It originally featured cross canopies of

Figure 111
The Arndale Centre in Jarrow, Tyne & Wear – now the Viking Centre – in a view of c. 1965. This precinct was built in 1959–61 and was clearly influenced by Stevenage.
[© The Francis Frith Collection]

Figure 112
The pedestrian town centre of Basildon, where the first
shops opened in 1958.
[Henk Snoek/RIBA Collections]

precisely the sort used at Stevenage, while these were also a feature of the Yate shopping centre near Bristol, built in phases between 1965 and 1970.

Pedestrian planning was increasingly adopted for later new town centres. For instance, in 1958 the London County Council planned a new pedestrian development at Hook in Hampshire. This scheme was ultimately abandoned, but those involved in its preparation – including Sir Isaac Hayward, leader of the LCC – visited Stevenage in 1959 to find inspiration, praising the 'outstanding' proportions of the buildings.[134] Meanwhile, at Basildon new town in Essex, the model of Stevenage was also taken up. The first phase of Basildon's pedestrian town centre was built slowly between 1956 and 1962 and included a market, a square containing public buildings and a church, plus a second square dominated by a tall and eye-catching block of flats (Fig. 112).

At Harlow, too, the new town centre was expanded with a pedestrian shopping precinct completed in *c.* 1967. The Broad Walk lined with shops extended to a pedestrian square and water gardens that served a civic centre (opened in 1963 and demolished in 2004). More ambitious was the experimental centre of Cumbernauld new town near Glasgow. Here, the architect Geoffrey Copcutt designed an enclosed shopping mall on a deck above the roads. Design work for this was undertaken in 1961–2 – a few years after a group from Cumbernauld had visited Stevenage – and it was constructed in 1963–7 (Fig. 113).[135]

The pace of pedestrian development grew from the early 1960s, when the government began to offer funding to urban areas which had not necessarily suffered much war damage but which required adaptation to motor traffic. A further boost came with the influential report Colin Buchanan prepared for the Ministry of Transport, *Traffic in Towns* (1963), which strongly advocated the separation of pedestrians and traffic. For Kenneth J. Robinson, writing in the *Sunday Times* in 1962, 'The town that separates cars from pedestrians is no longer a Utopian dream'.[136] He cited as three 'superb examples' the pedestrian town centres at Coventry, Stevenage and Cumbernauld. Britain was acknowledged to be 'leading the way' in this area. In 1962 'hundreds of foreign planners and architects came to this country to visit tomorrow's towns ... They walked through traffic-free shopping squares, after leaving their cars on roof-top car parks which are never overcrowded'.[137]

Local authorities increasingly used their powers of compulsory purchase to redevelop older buildings and create entirely new pedestrian centres on the Stevenage model. Demolition on this scale was highly controversial. For instance, at Blackburn in Lancashire, 15 acres of the town centre were cleared between 1962 and 1964 to create a 500,000 sq. ft (46,452m²) shopping centre and market hall. Other open-air schemes of these years included the Merrion Centre in Leeds (1962–4), the Whitgift Centre in Croydon, London (1969), and The Walks, a shopping precinct in Basingstoke (1968–72). All of these were subsequently covered over with roofs.

In Britain, the first covered shopping centres were designed in 1960, with contemporaneous schemes for the Elephant and Castle in London and the Bull Ring in Birmingham, both opened in 1964 (Fig. 114). Before long, covered centres of this type were being opened throughout Britain, among them the earliest indoor Arndale Centre at Cross Gates, Leeds (opened in 1967), and Nottingham's Victoria Centre (1965–72). As covered shopping centres rose in popularity in Britain, open-air shopping precincts came to be criticised by some

Figure 113
The innovative town centre of Cumbernauld new town in
Scotland, built in 1963–7.
[Architectural Press Archive/RIBA Collections]

Figure 114
Birmingham's Bull Ring shopping centre on its opening
day, 29 May 1964.
[JLP01/10/00149]

as 'windy deserts'.[138] However, the tide of pedestrianisation continued. Applications to convert historic streets to pedestrian zones were made thick and fast from the late 1960s – the earliest to be implemented in Britain included London Street in Norwich (1967) and London's Carnaby Street (1973).

Today, pedestrian planning is considered the norm for most town and city shopping streets, with concerns greater than ever before about the environmental and other damage caused by motor vehicles. Even enclosed shopping malls are now falling out of favour – some are being replaced by partly open pedestrian streets on the Stevenage model, as with Birmingham's Bull Ring (first phase of rebuilding completed in 2003) and Nottingham's Broadmarsh (where new building began in 2021). In this context, the development at Stevenage town centre seems pioneering and far-sighted indeed, for it was in the vanguard of an enormously significant trend in planning. The town centre's pedestrian layout reflected the rising problem of traffic and vehicular pollution in the post-war years, but Stevenage's planners had no idea that this issue would continue to escalate over the course of the century and into the 2000s, both in Britain and internationally. This makes Stevenage of continued relevance for a modern audience.

Historic and communal significance

Stevenage occupies a special place in popular culture, both locally and nationally. As the first new town designated, it was part of a dream for a better Britain – one that could move forwards after the heavy losses of the Second World War, allowing young families to put congested and blitzed urban areas behind them and find employment and contentment in an entirely new environment. The new town's early years were fraught with challenges and delays. However, when the first phases of work were completed, including the shopping precinct, all eyes turned to Stevenage and what had been achieved.

The architectural importance of Stevenage's shopping precinct has been discussed above, but it is also notable as a key triumph for the local people, who fought for the scheme in the face of opposition from capital interest, big business and government. As the architect David Rixson has noted, 'blood was spilled' during this vicious debate, but all ultimately agreed that the end result was worth it, with many opponents of the pedestrian development later admitting that they had been wrong.[139]

As the central focus for Stevenage new town, the town centre has played a major part in the lives of many locals. In this aspect as in others, the area proved immediately successful. It originally provided accommodation for 300 families, in addition to the thousands of visitors each year. Tom Hampson of the Development Corporation wrote in 1959 that

> Even in its present state, the social significance of the Town Centre is apparent. It is not only a shopping centre. People do sit around in the Town Square; they meet and talk there; children play there. The few cafés so far established are well used. It is already becoming the hub of the town, and it may well become the centre of a region.[140]

In particular, the Town Square and the platform have been a social magnet, being used for exhibitions, dances, meetings, celebrations and protests (Fig. 115). *The Times* newspaper commented that the platform was intended to be used 'for speeches, concerts, and sitting in the sun', while an official at the Development Corporation felt that the Town Square as a whole had enormous possibilities, capable of use as 'a vast auditorium for public spectacles and special occasions', akin to a continental piazza or a village green.[141] It was here that the Queen stood on opening the town centre in April 1959, with crowds gathered all around.

Elsewhere in the town centre, buildings with strong communal associations include the library, the Edward the Confessor pub at 1 Town Square, the church, the indoor market, the Mecca dance hall and the youth centre. The latter two venues were the focus for entertainment for decades, hosting concerts by major bands and artists including David Bowie, the Rolling Stones, The Who, Cream and Thin Lizzy. Wider interest in Stevenage was enhanced by the promotional material issued by the Development Corporation, and also by the film *Here We Go Round the Mulberry Bush* (1967). This coming-of-age comedy, directed by Clive Donner and starring Barry Evans, was shot entirely in Stevenage and was released to some critical acclaim. Among various locations featured are the Town Square, Queensway, the Long Ship pub and the Bowes Lyon House youth centre.

Figure 115
Members of the public viewing an exhibition of works by local
artists on the platform in the Town Square, c. 1960.
[Stevenage Museum]

Daneshill House is worthy of special note. Although the original designs for the town centre were produced at Stevenage Development Corporation's former base at Aston House, controversially demolished in the 1960s, it was at Daneshill House that Vincent, his colleagues and his successors produced designs from 1961 to 1980. Even after setting up as a freelance consultant in 1962, Vincent continued to have dedicated offices in Daneshill House. The block was at the heart of the new town both physically and functionally and is a monument to the achievements of both the Corporation and Stevenage Borough Council, which has occupied the building since the early 1980s.

Level of survival

Stevenage remained almost exactly as built at the time of the dissolution of the Development Corporation in 1980. Since then, as has been shown in Chapter 6, there have been a number of changes and alterations, including the demolition of three buildings designed under Leonard Vincent. These reflect in part the diversification of freehold property ownership from that point, but they are also due to the building of edge-of-town retail and leisure parks and the challenging economic climate of the late 1900s and early 2000s.

However, at the time of writing, Stevenage town centre still survives largely as completed by Leonard Vincent and the Development Corporation. This includes numerous smaller elements of the townscape, such as windows, signs, coloured panels, trees and some of the cross canopies, as well as the buildings themselves (Figs 116 and 117). With the exception of the Head Post Office, the bowling centre and the bus garage, all the key components of the 1950s scheme still remain – including the shopping precinct, the bus station, Daneshill House, the Mecca dance hall, The Towers point block and the grade II-listed church. This level of survival allows for a ready understanding and appreciation of the accomplishments of Leonard Vincent and others at the Development Corporation, and the architectural impact achieved in the 1950s and 1960s.

Also surviving are most of the structures built as part of the 1960s extensions to the shopping precinct – including the two-storey bridge, the former Littlewoods store and the north part of Queensway – and all the major

Figure 116
Coloured panels beneath the windows on the east side of Queensway. All date from 1958 except the blue panels (above Boots), which are sympathetic replacements of c. 2017.
[DP233277 and DP233283, Derek Kendall]

Figure 117
Notably, the 1950s cross canopies of Market Place all survive, with original lettering.
[DP233300, Derek Kendall]

buildings constructed on the peripheries of the centre in the 1950s and 1960s. These include Swingate House, Brickdale House, the outpatients' clinic, the library and health centre, the police station, Southgate House, the fire and ambulance station and the youth centre. Slightly later but still notable surviving structures are the 1970s multistorey car park on St George's Way, the arts and leisure centre, the shops in The Forum, the railway station and the elevated walkway. Altogether, this represents almost the entire scheme devised by Leonard Vincent.

Certainly, Stevenage town centre is much better preserved overall than the town centre of any other British new town. Harlow, Crawley, Basildon and Bracknell have all been the subject of significant alteration and demolition over the past three decades. Stevenage town centre is as impressive as its major (and slightly earlier) comparator – the Upper Precinct at Coventry (listed grade II in 2018) – while the slightly later Lower Precinct has been far more radically altered and was roofed over in 2001–2 (Fig. 118). No other British town centre pedestrian precinct of the 1950s or 1960s has such architectural interest or survives to the same degree.

Figure 118
Photograph of 2008 showing Coventry's Upper Precinct in the foreground (the modern glazed escalator was installed in c. 1993, removed in 2019) and the Lower Precinct beyond (with glass roof added in 2001–2).
[DP059655, James O. Davies]

8

The future of Stevenage town centre

As the preceding chapters have illustrated, Stevenage new town is of international significance in the context of its historic environment and the history of town planning. It is a place of 'firsts'. It was the first of Britain's new towns to be designated as such following the Second World War (in 1946). It was also the first formally designed pedestrianised town centre in the country, and it incorporated many other innovations besides.

As can be seen by any visitor, the core of the town centre remains notable for its cohesion and architectural unity. Its masterplanning and architecture embody many broader aspects of the immediate post-war period, including a sense of clean, crisp modernity and the incorporation of public art in prominent locations, a feature common to many new towns. In the town centre, the architectural design of the structures was, like the masterplanning, consistent and regular, owing to the centralised influence of the Development Corporation and Leonard Vincent. The planned, coherent and integral nature of Stevenage's development means its significance is embodied in all the surviving buildings and spaces in the town centre – albeit to varying degrees.

Outside the town centre, Stevenage's neighbourhoods were designed to contain all the immediate necessities its new communities would require, while also providing direct, easy access to the centre and employment zone in the west, via a combination of a comprehensively planned road network and around 26 miles of segregated cycle lanes (Fig. 119). Ancient woodland was incorporated to break up the developed areas and provide access to natural green space, alongside the wonderful and hard-won amenity of Fairlands Valley Park (Fig. 120). Overall, Stevenage's character, despite some slightly threadbare areas, reminds us of a period when there was a renewed focus on how planning could provide a better, healthier and more comfortable life for people of any background – many of whom in Stevenage had moved from substandard or bombed-out accommodation in inner-city London.

Stevenage new town is therefore a historic place that can, without cliché, be described as 'unique'. Although it shares a number of characteristics with other new towns, nowhere else in the United Kingdom can these be described as 'the first'. Nowhere else have the original principles, layout and architectural character of the place as originally conceived by its development corporation design team survived as intact and legible as they do in Stevenage. Few other places in Britain can claim to have had such an influence on post-war planning

View looking west along Park Place, showing the 1960s blocks heavily remodelled in 2017–18 to designs by Gardner Stewart Architects.
[DP233408, Derek Kendall]

Figure 119
Cycle lanes and pedestrian paths beneath Six Hills Way, to the south of the town centre, in an early 1960s photograph.
[© Crown copyright, DAC01/03/009]

Figure 120
The 120-acre Fairlands Valley Park in the heart of Stevenage.
[DP247607, Patricia Payne]

discourse, and despite being afflicted by similar problems that have dogged other urban centres across England, overall Stevenage is one of the most successful of the new towns to be constructed.

Challenges

Now, in the third decade of the 21st century, Stevenage faces perhaps the greatest period of change since the last phases of its construction under the auspices of the Development Corporation. It faces the prospect of considerable population growth, with new urban extensions to its north and west planned, as well as large-scale regeneration and change at its heart, providing many thousands of new homes. This change will happen in the broader context of enormous shifts in consumer behaviour and expectations, the need to combat climate change and the need to accommodate the pressure of an expanding population. Stevenage's capacity to manage this change will be tested, particularly from the perspective of maintaining its unique and special sense of place and conserving its historic environment.

Stevenage is no stranger to difficult times and has faced considerable challenges since maturing into an established town. These have only evolved, rather than diminished, and of course Stevenage has weathered the same changes to the economic and particularly retail environments over the last 40 or so years that have often resulted in the decline of town centres elsewhere. For example, at Stevenage, despite attempts by the planning authority to limit the effects, the 'out of town' Roaring Meg business park at Monkswood that was developed during the 1980s and 1990s has consistently competed with the town centre for footfall and has often attracted large brand-name stores. At the same time, the increasing dependency of the growing local population on the private car for transport, as well as the relatively poor pedestrian connectivity into the town centre created by the original Master Plan's design, meant the business parks had a natural advantage over the town centre.

Regrettably, this undermined the remarkable success story that Stevenage's pedestrian town centre had previously been. As has been discussed elsewhere in this book, the precinct once attracted large numbers of shoppers to enjoy its vehicle-free environment, confounding the early critics who said that such a town centre would

Figure 121
The south section of Queensway in 2021, during the
COVID-19 pandemic.
[DP233319, Derek Kendall]

not be viable. More recently still, however, and certainly over the decade 2010–20, the ever-growing impact of online sales on traditional 'high street' retail businesses has undoubtedly contributed to a prolonged difficult and challenging period for the town centre's economic vitality. At the time of writing, the COVID-19 pandemic and its restrictions have only enhanced this trend (Fig. 121).

Other factors, as described in earlier chapters, have concurrently reduced the quality of the town centre environment. The dissolution of the Development Corporation and the dispersal of its assets to private investors meant that a degree of coordinating oversight and control was lost regarding the development of the town centre. At the same time, reduced funding for local government and a shift in focus towards inner-city renewal led to a period of political disinterest in the fate of the post-war new towns nationally. This exacerbated existing local issues including under-investment by private landowners, the changing needs and aspirations of people and businesses, structures aging at similar rates, and increasing numbers of vacant buildings.

Overall, by the early 2000s, the centre of Stevenage was a place that was obviously in decline, was unattractive to spend time in and badly needed investment. Now, however, after a number of abortive schemes were halted by the advent of the Global Financial Crisis, Stevenage is on the cusp of receiving the scale of investment it needs.

Opportunities

Stevenage is remarkably fortunate, in that it has many natural attributes that should underpin its success. It is probably the most favourably located of all the new towns except perhaps Milton Keynes: it is close to London, connected to major north–south road and rail transport routes and in relatively close proximity to two international airports. Unlike neighbouring Welwyn-Hatfield new town, its historic anchor aerospace engineering industry has survived the industrial contraction of the late 20th century and remains at the centre of the European space programme. Stevenage is also the home of one of the leading global pharmaceutical companies and the country's leading wine business. COVID-19 notwithstanding, Stevenage boasts enviable employment figures above the national average.[142]

Stevenage's residents have superb access to green space as a result of the 1946 Master Plan, which conceived the retention of mature woodland as well as the lakes in Fairlands Valley. The town's network of cycle paths, although presently under-appreciated, largely remains intact and the town's regular road network, while the cause of one of its key issues, also offers great potential for the future of connected autonomous vehicles and other sustainable modes of transport.[143]

Finally, of course, Stevenage's modernist built heritage is a great asset and bonus at a time when 20th-century heritage is becoming ever more popular. With careful nurturing, investment and reinstatement, the town centre – arranged around the core public space of the Town Square and punctuated by the listed clock tower and embellished by public art – should boast a singular character and aesthetic appeal, complemented by Leonard Vincent's high-quality, human-scale townscape and architectural form.

This provides solid foundations for a vibrant and thriving town centre rightly proud of its heritage and that celebrates its history as a place of positivity, dynamism and growth. This is, of course, the attractive vision and narrative that

Stevenage Borough Council share and use to underpin their £1 billion proposals and the recent (2021) award of £37.5 million funding through the government's Towns Fund programme. At the heart of this is the Stevenage Town Investment Plan; this emphasises the importance of culture and heritage and includes funding towards enhancements to the public realm, improved cycle connectivity and a heritage trail. In addition, the Plan hopes to draw in funding for a centrally located new towns heritage centre aiming to celebrate the unique history of Stevenage and the architectural, planning and social history of the new towns movement. As with any regeneration plan, there is a need to imagine a compelling new future, but there is always a cost to consider.

The regeneration of Stevenage town centre

It has become clear that in its current form the new town centre does not have the capacity to service the needs of Stevenage's future population as a retail centre. In addition to issues of connectivity, a lack of housing in the centre means that it is lacking a 'critical mass' of people living within easy, walkable distance. The area is thus unable to take full advantage of its potential for a more mixed economy that enjoys a greater presence of leisure and hospitality uses (in noticeable contrast to Old Stevenage to the north and the Leisure Park to the west).

To remedy this, Stevenage Borough Council has purchased and regained control of a small number of historic Development Corporation assets (including 1–29 Town Square), and has been successful in gaining significant funding to bring forward substantial town centre regeneration proposals. These were launched as part of the Stevenage Central Framework in summer 2015, followed by incorporation into planning policy within the Stevenage Borough Local Plan 2011–31, adopted in 2019.

The most recent component of the regeneration scheme is known as 'SG1', and involves the Council working in partnership with the retail development company Reef Group and the development and construction firm Mace. Once completed, the proposals will comprise almost 2,000 new homes; new areas of public realm and landscaping; mixed use and commercial space; a new pedestrian shopping street (Fig. 122); and at the heart of the town centre a public

Figure 122
Design scheme for The Boulevard, a new pedestrian
shopping street due to be built between the Town
Square and the railway station.
[Courtesy of Mace and Stevenage Borough Council]

services 'hub', which will include a heritage centre, a new public library and health facilities. This element of the regeneration will affect large areas of the town centre, especially in its south and west parts, and will bring residential accommodation at considerable scale into the zone for the first time, in contrast to the principles set out in the town's original master plans.

On the face of it, regeneration is great news for Stevenage. It will create many new opportunities for employment, provide local people with much needed housing accommodation and support the vitality of the town centre as a whole through a substantially increased local population, who will make use of the new and historic public spaces and the services, bringing an estimated spending power of £38.6 million per annum.[144] The thorny issue of how to support the town centre economy despite the aforementioned lack of pedestrian connectivity is being addressed. There is no substantial pre-existing residential population that will be displaced. In addition, the Stevenage Development Board, set up in 2020, makes clear that Stevenage's architectural heritage has been a design inspiration for the SG1 project (and others also in development), noting that

> one of the key principles of our regeneration scheme is to make sure that it
> is still recognisable, treasuring and protecting the historic landmarks and
> countryside that make Stevenage unique. To ensure this is the case,
> inspiration for many of the new buildings and developments draws on
> Stevenage's rich culture and heritage, and we will be working to make sure
> that there will be no unsightly juxtaposition between the old and new.[145]

Broadly speaking, then, there is a great deal to be positive about regarding the future of Stevenage town centre, and Historic England supports the principle of the regeneration. Many aspects of the scheme are unequivocally welcome, and will – if they come to fruition – breathe new life into long-term vacant spaces and buildings in the conservation area, including some of the most important buildings that surround the Town Square and comprise the core of the area originally designated as a conservation area in 1988, enhancing its appearance.

Already there has been considerable development as part of the regeneration programme, undertaken to varying levels of sensitivity to the historic townscape context. This has included changes to the public realm at Littlewoods Square in 2017 (work which involved the removal of original 1960s cross canopies) (*see* Fig. 53) and the expansion of the railway station in 2020. In 2019 work began on the 'Queensway North' project, a £50 million development focusing on the disused former Marks & Spencer premises and the adjoining parade (Fig. 123). This will see the area repurposed to provide mixed-use residential, commercial and leisure activity. Stevenage Borough Council has also completed a major refurbishment of 21–29 Town Square. This has provided new upper-floor commercial space, while the ground-floor spaces have been refitted to attract cafés and restaurants (Fig. 124). In the Town Square itself, work to the public realm has included new paving and seating, utilising materials and designs that

Figure 123
Artwork for the scheme in north Queensway, due to be completed in 2021.
[Courtesy of Reef and Stevenage Borough Council]

Figure 124
The north side of the Town Square following the completion of refurbishment works undertaken in 2020–1.
[DP233339, Derek Kendall]

Figure 125
The east part of the Town Square showing public realm works undertaken in 2020–1.
[DP233262, Derek Kendall]

are broadly sympathetic (Fig. 125). New lighting columns reminiscent of the long-since lost originals are particularly effective (*see* Fig. 127).

Although in many places the design quality of Stevenage's regeneration has been high, some of the projects have compromised the historic integrity of the town centre. This is exemplified by three private developments. Southgate House was reopened as 'Vista Tower' in 2016, having been heavily remodelled in its conversion from office to residential use (Fig. 126), and the same process was undertaken using Permitted Development rights at the earliest block of

Figure 126
*Southgate House was renamed Vista Tower following
a remodelling of 2014–16.*
[DP278147, Patricia Payne]

Figure 127
*Joy Ride on the elevated platform in 2021, with new
lighting in the background, sympathetically modelled on
the 1950s originals.*
[DP233343, Derek Kendall]

Brickdale House, reopened in 2017. Also in that year, work began on the radical remodelling of the early 1960s buildings of Park Place, to designs by Gardner Stewart Architects (*see* p. 128). The existing three-storey premises were heightened by an additional three storeys, the accommodation providing extra town-centre residential space, but nonetheless rendering the buildings unrecognisable as 1960s architecture.

The proposals for future change will also, however, result in the complete demolition of a number of buildings and structures that are fundamental to the historic composition of Stevenage town centre. At present, the Town Square overall survives as created in the late 1950s: it is framed by buildings on three sides and the bus station on the west, and has at its centre the so-called 'Joy Ride Platform'. This supports Franta Belsky's grade II-listed *Joy Ride* sculpture and its plinth and, despite some unfortunate alterations undertaken in the 1990s, comprises an integral part of the original town centre plan, as set out by Leonard Vincent and his team (Fig. 127). Under the SG1 proposals, the platform is due to be demolished to make way for a more accessible public space comprising a 'garden square', with room for cafés, bars or restaurants around its edges (Figs 128 and 129).

The *Joy Ride* sculpture, which is to be retained and relocated, symbolises the vision of Stevenage as a new town, a mother and child representing old and new (*see* pp. 40–1). The platform is both functional and aesthetic: it encloses public toilets and was used as a means of breaking up the large, sloping Town Square area, and creating visual and spatial interest and variety. Historically, it also hosted dances and other public events (*see* Fig. 115). The relative heights, placement and alignment between the platform (in its original form), the *Joy Ride* sculpture and the clock tower and pool (also listed grade II), as well as their collective relationship to adjacent spaces, comprise part of a coherent whole. This important composition will be lost.

Other important elements of Stevenage's historic environment that will be demolished are Daneshill House and the Mecca dance hall. Both of these are due to make way for a new pedestrian route, 'The Boulevard', while the car park on the site of the former bowling centre and Swingate House to the north will be redeveloped as the 'North Quarter', a new residential zone. Other structures that will be lost include the former Barclays Bank (of 1957–8) and the modern Plaza complex in the Town Square. Additionally, the block comprising 1–19 Town

Figure 128
Design scheme for refurbishment of the Town Square and new buildings to its south-west, west and north-west.
[Courtesy of Mace and Stevenage Borough Council]

Figure 129
The proposals for regeneration of the Town Square.
[Courtesy of Mace and Stevenage Borough Council]

Square (of 1957–8, but not within the conservation area) is due to be redeveloped, along with the bus station, which will be relocated to the west of Danestrete as part of the creation of a new 'garden square' (Fig. 130).

Buildings original to the conception of Stevenage's development at the south of the town centre – including the outpatients' clinic, library and health centre, and police station – will also be demolished, to be redeveloped as housing and landscaped public space at 'Southgate Park'. In addition, the regeneration framework has the ambitions to replace the swimming pool and Bowes Lyon House youth centre on St George's Way with new facilities. Much of the new construction proposed for the town centre is overall of a far larger scale than the

Figure 130
The 1950s bus station and 1–19 Town Square are due to
be redeveloped as part of the regeneration scheme.
[DP278909, Patricia Payne]

historic core of Stevenage, which was – as has been described – specified by the Development Corporation team to be generally no greater than three storeys in height.

Taken together, the proposals represent a wholesale change to the town centre, and they will result in the loss of major aspects that contribute to its composition and the story of its development. At the point of providing planning advice, Historic England reluctantly concluded that despite many positive aspects of the proposals and obvious design references to Stevenage's aesthetic being made, the cumulative level of harm to the significance of the Town Square Conservation Area, and the listed buildings within it, is extremely high. Regrettably, Historic England therefore objected to the proposals despite recognising the importance of the regeneration programme to Stevenage. Despite this, planning permission for the scheme was granted by Stevenage Borough Council in October 2020.

Conclusion

The long-awaited regeneration of Stevenage town centre will undoubtedly result in a very different Stevenage to the one that readers will be familiar with. Once realised, the regeneration programme for the town aims to draw in over £1 billion of investment and should indeed counter the narrative of decline that has perhaps unfairly dogged Stevenage's recent history, alongside that of its contemporary new towns. The regeneration is of course intended to reflect Stevenage's unique history and proud past; Councillor Sharon Taylor, Leader of Stevenage Borough Council, has stated that 'Our approach is about celebrating the very best of the history of the town, enhancing the conservation areas, breathing new life into older buildings, and bringing in new, sympathetic buildings to cater for the next 75 years of the New Town story'.[146]

Nonetheless, despite the predominantly positive story of Stevenage's regeneration, it is clear that change will come at the cost of losing some of the town's most prominent structures and buildings. These represent and witnessed the very beginnings of Stevenage new town as a historic place. Although in some cases now vacant and in poor condition, they contribute fundamentally to its character and integrity, and their loss diminishes Stevenage's status as the most intact of the post-war new towns. It also comes at a time when many of the other new towns, such as Basildon, Hatfield and Harlow, have themselves been the subject of significant change.

The challenge of regeneration is always to imagine a bright future and bring about transformative change in a way that nevertheless reflects and respects the history, integrity, architecture and broader qualities of a place. However, in Stevenage – a pioneering, influential and currently intact post-war development – will such change come at the price of losing part of the town's historic significance? This remains to be seen.

Appendix: Timeline of town centre construction under Stevenage Development Corporation (1954–80)

1954	autumn	Work begins on road network (including Danestrete)
1955		Work begins on bus station, Danestrete
1956	June	On-site prefabrication begins for shopping precinct
		Work on bus station completed around now (but not opened until October 1958; *see below*)
	July	Laying of foundation stone of St George's Church, St George's Way
	September	Main building contract for town centre begins, with work on south side of the Town Square
	November	Work begins on north side of the Town Square
	December	Work begins on east side of the Town Square
1957	January	Work begins on south part of Queensway, extending into Market Place, north up Queensway and into Park Place
		Work begins on north-west arm of the Town Square
	late	Work begins on bus garage, Danestrete
1958	January	Shopfitting begins with the Co-op in the Town Square
	June	First shops opened (Lavells and Co-op)
	c. June	Completion of work on north-west arm of the Town Square (nos 1–19)
	July	The Town Square comes into use
	July–December	Further multiples, banks and shops opened
	July	Opening of Lloyds at 3–5 Town Square – the first bank to begin trading in the new town centre
	August	Work begins on clock tower, pool and platform in the Town Square
		Work begins around now on Town Centre Gardens
	September	*Joy Ride* unveiled on the platform in the Town Square
		Barclays opened at 2–4 Town Square
	October	Official opening of bus station, Danestrete
		Opening of Westgate, East Gate and The Quadrant car parks
	November	Work begins on Head Post Office, Danestrete
	December	Unveiling of clock tower
		Opening of Daneshill car park
1959		Work begins on police station, Southgate
	April	Official opening of the town centre by the Queen
		Opening of bus garage, Danestrete

	May	Opening of east part of Market Square car park
		Work begins around now on county library and county health centre, Southgate
	autumn	Opening of Edward the Confessor public house, 1 Town Square
	September	Work begins on Daneshill House, Danestrete
		Completion of Head Post Office
	October	Work begins on Langley House, Southgate
		Opening of west part of Market Square car park
	November	Trading begins in the open market, Market Square
	December	Official opening of Head Post Office
1960	early	Work begins around now on outpatients' clinic, Southgate
	March	Work begins on The Towers, Southgate
	May	Work begins on the Mecca dance hall, Danestrete
	August	Opening of Swingate car park
	October	Foundation stone of Mecca dance hall laid
		Langley House completed
		Police station and health centre in Southgate in full use from this month
	November	Consecration and opening of St George's Church
1961	January	Completion of Daneshill House, Danestrete
		Opening of county library, Southgate
		Opening of police station, Southgate
		Work begins on fire and ambulance station, St George's Way
	April	Site work begins for extension of shopping precinct
		Opening of outpatients' clinic, Southgate
		Work begins on swimming pool, St George's Way
	May	Opening of county health centre, Southgate
	summer	Completion of Town Centre Gardens (official opening: January 1962)
	July	Government call for economies in public expenditure – some town centre works temporarily put on hold
		Work begins on Swingate House, Danestrete, for Lloyds Bank Branches Clearing Centre
	autumn	Midland Bank opens on ground floor of Daneshill House
	October	Opening of Mecca dance hall, Danestrete
	November	Opening around now of Central Garage, Danestrete
1962	June	Final scheme for civic centre approved around now

	July	Announcement of proposals for Stevenage expansion
		Opening of fire and ambulance station, St George's Way
	August	Work begins in earnest on extension of shopping precinct
		Press launch and public opening of Ambassador Lanes bowling centre, Danestrete (official opening: September)
	October	Opening of swimming pool, St George's Way
	November	Completion of sorting office at Head Post Office, Danestrete
	December	Completion of Swingate House, Danestrete
1963	March	Completion of The Towers, Southgate
	April	Work begins on Southgate House, St George's Way
	October	Opening of Littlewoods in north extension of Queensway
	Oct.–Dec.	Opening of shops in north extension of Queensway
	December	Unofficial opening of Clarion Club in two-storey bridge, Queensway (official opening: February 1964)
1964		Installation of aluminium sculpture by Peter Lyon on west face of 21–23 Town Square
	March	Work begins on youth centre (Bowes Lyon House), St George's Way
		Work begins on Brickdale House, Danestrete
	April	County library reopened following extension (completed late February)
	May	Opening of Chinese restaurant ('Blossom Garden') in two-storey bridge, Queensway
	June	Foundation stone laid for youth centre
	September	Completion of Southgate House, St George's Way
	December	Completion around now of 22 shops with offices above in Park Place
1965	April	Opening of youth centre (Bowes Lyon House)
1966	February	First phase of works at Brickdale House completed
	April	Bowling centre seriously damaged by fire
	October	Opening of the Long Ship pub and restaurant at base of Southgate House, St George's Way
1967		Work begins on north section of Queensway
	February	Reopening of bowling centre
1968		Completion around now of stage two of Brickdale House
1969		Completion of Lytton Way
	October	Sainsbury's opens in north section of Queensway
1970	April	Marks & Spencer opens in north section of Queensway
		Work begins on Grampian Hotel
1971	March	Work begins on multistorey car park, St George's Way
	July	Work begins on commercial block on The Forum at north-east of town centre

	September	Work begins around now on new railway station, Lytton Way
1972		Work begins on Manulife House, St George's Way
	March	Work begins on magistrates' court, Danesgate
		Unveiling of untitled sculpture by José de Alberdi, Queensway
1973		Underpasses completed beneath newly dual-carriagewayed St George's Way, with relief sculptures by William Mitchell
	February	Opening of Grampian Hotel, The Forum
	c. spring	Opening of magistrates' court, Danesgate
	July	Stevenage new town railway station opens to passengers with elevated walkway over Lytton Way (a day after the station at Old Stevenage is closed) (official opening: September)
	October	Opening of Manulife House, St George's Way
	November	Opening of ABC cinema and Tesco in north-east block, The Forum
	December	Completion of multistorey car park off St George's Way and opening of covered market on ground floor
1974		Stage three of Brickdale House completed
		Police station moved from Southgate to new building on Lytton Way
	February	Unveiling of plaque to Lewis Silkin on west side of clock tower
	June	Foundation stone of arts and leisure centre laid
1975		Elevated walkway from railway station to town centre completed
		Opening of C&A, The Forum
	November	Arts and leisure centre opened for business (official opening: February 1976)
1976		Opening of BHS, The Forum
		Completion around now of block on south side of The Forum, opposite Tesco and ABC cinema
1978		Opening of skatepark to east of youth centre (Bowes Lyon House)

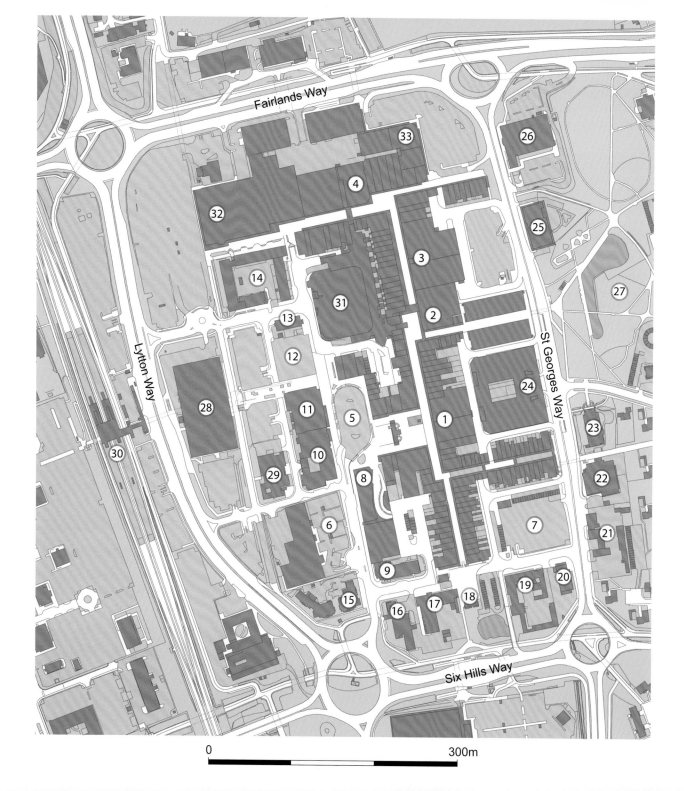

Fairlands Way

Lytton Way

St Georges Way

Six Hills Way

0   300m

Gazetteer

1 Shopping precinct – phase I

The 'core' of the pedestrian town centre, built in 1956–9 to designs by Leonard Vincent and his team at SDC. It comprised the blocks of Queensway, Market Place, the Town Square and part of Park Place, with 108 shops below and offices and flats/maisonettes above. The clock tower and elevated platform in the Town Square were both completed in the second half of 1958. The precinct is now designated a conservation area, but there are current proposals for change, especially around the Town Square.

2 Shopping precinct – phase II

The first extension of the shopping precinct, built in 1962–4 to designs by Leonard Vincent and his team at SDC. It provided around 10 commercial premises with offices above in Queensway and 22 shops with offices above in Park Place. The new buildings included a Littlewoods (opened October 1963) and the two-storey bridge crossing Queensway. The buildings of Park Place were heavily remodelled and extended in 2017–18.

3 Shopping precinct – phase III

This phase was designed under Leonard Vincent at SDC in 1961, but not built until 1967–70. It involved the extension of Queensway to reach The Forum at the north. New shops included Sainsbury's (opened October 1969) and Marks & Spencer (opened April 1970). Office space was provided above the commercial premises. A programme of rebuilding on the east side of this part of Queensway was initiated in 2019.

4 Shopping precinct – phase IV

The buildings of The Forum were constructed in 1970–6. They were designed by freelance architects in liaison with Leonard Vincent as consultant to SDC. The new facilities included a commercial block for Tesco and an ABC cinema (1971–3; demolished c. 1995), the Grampian Hotel (1970–3; now the Ibis), a branch of C&A (opened 1975) and a BHS department store (opened 1976).

5 Bus station

The bus station, with the car parks, was a fundamental component of Stevenage's pedestrian scheme. It was laid out in 1955–6 under George Hardy, Chief Engineer of SDC, between Danestrete and the Town Square. The area was used for construction and the storage of building materials until its formal opening in October 1958. The bus station was enlarged and remodelled in the 1970s and 1980s. The location of the bus station is due to be moved and its current site redeveloped.

6 Bus garage (site of)

The bus garage was begun around late 1957 and opened in April 1959. It was built to designs by Thomas Bilbow (1893–1983), Chief Architect of the London Transport Executive, and comprised a single-storey office range and a tall garage block behind. The bus garage was demolished in 1993 and replaced in 1994–5 by a retail unit, now occupied by Matalan. There are current plans for redevelopment of the site as housing.

7 Surface car parks

The provision of adequate car parking was key to ensuring the success of Stevenage's pedestrian precinct. By 1963 there were seven main surface car parks in the town centre. The earliest were opened in 1958–9: at Westgate, East Gate, the west side of Danestrete, the Market Square and The Quadrant (off Southgate). Further car parks were added in the early 1960s, including the Swingate car park and the car park at Marsh Gate. The East Gate car park contains the boiler house of c. 1958, built to power the shopping precinct. There are current plans for redevelopment of the East Gate, Quadrant and Marsh Gate car parks, which are the only car parks of the 1950s and 1960s to survive.

The boiler house of c. 1958, built to power the shopping precinct. It is a notable survival at the north-west corner of the East Gate car park – now without its tall chimney.
[DP275711, James O. Davies]

8 Head Post Office (site of)

The Head Post Office was begun in late 1958 and completed in September 1959. The building was designed for the Ministry of Works by Leonard Vincent and his team at SDC. It was a curtain-walled structure of four floors; a low sorting office was added to the rear in 1961–2. Both buildings were demolished in 1999 to make way for The Plaza, a retail and leisure scheme which is now due to be redeveloped.

9 Langley House (site of)

Langley House was an office block built to designs by Leonard Vincent and his team at SDC. It was begun in October 1959 as a speculative office development and following completion in 1960 was occupied by British Railways. It was demolished in 2003 and replaced by a Holiday Inn hotel, opened 2004.

10 Daneshill House

Daneshill House is a seven-storey, curtain-walled office block built from September 1959 to January 1961 to designs by Leonard Vincent at SDC. It was constructed as the offices of SDC itself, with commercial units on the ground floor leased to Midland Bank (now HSBC). Following the dissolution of SDC, the building was altered and extended in the early 1980s as the offices of Stevenage Borough Council. It is due to be demolished.

11 Mecca dance hall

The Mecca dance hall or 'Locarno' in Danestrete was a major entertainment amenity for Stevenage, begun in October 1960 and opened in October 1961. It was designed by Leonard Vincent and his team at SDC and contained a large ballroom. The building is now a Mecca bingo hall, though

The former Mecca dance hall in Danestrete, now a bingo hall, in a photograph of 2020. [DP278095, Patricia Payne]

retains its former ballroom with balcony. It is due to be redeveloped.

12 Bowling centre (site of)

The Ambassador Lanes bowling centre was designed under Leonard Vincent at SDC. It was a low building, begun in autumn 1961 and completed in August 1962. Damaged by fire in 1966, the centre was rebuilt and reopened in 1967 but closed as a venue in c. 2002. It was then demolished and replaced by a surface car park. Its site is due to be redeveloped.

13 Swingate House

This office block was designed under Leonard Vincent at SDC and built in 1961–2 for the Lloyds Bank Branches Clearing Centre. In 1968 it was taken on as offices by SDC and was also used by Stevenage Borough Council. A minor remodelling was undertaken in 1982. The building is due to be demolished.

14 Brickdale House

This was known as the 'Crown offices' development, built to house various government departments, including the Land Registry. It was designed by Ministry

architects and later the Property Services Agency and was built in stages – 1964–6, c. 1967–8, 1973–4 and 1986–7. The earliest block was heavily reworked as housing, completed in 2017.

15 Central Garage (site of)

This petrol station and car showroom was built in 1960–1 for Shell-Mex BP, to designs by the architect Max Lock (1909–88). The building was demolished in 2005 and has been replaced by blocks of apartments.

16 Outpatients' clinic

This clinic, now used by the NHS, was built in 1960–1 for the North-West Metropolitan Regional Hospital Board. It was designed by consultant architect Peter Dunham (1911–97). The building survives well, but is due to be demolished.

17 County library and county health centre

A building of two parts – the west side accommodates the county library and the east side the county health centre. It was designed by the architects of Hertfordshire County Council and built in 1959–60. The

The county library and health centre in 2020, with The Towers point block beyond. [DP278133, Patricia Payne]

library was greatly extended in 1961–4. The building is due to be redeveloped.

18 The Towers

This 16-storey residential point block on Southgate was built in 1960–3 to designs by Leonard Vincent and his team at SDC. It forms a focal point in the townscape, and closes the south end of Queensway. The gardens include a sculpture, *Three Figures*, by David Noble (1963). The Towers is the only building on the south side of Southgate due to be retained in the proposed scheme of works.

19 Police station and garages

The police station was built in 1959–60 to designs by Hertfordshire County Council Architect's Department. It was served by an

The Long Ship pub opened in 1966 at the base of Southgate House, with its large mosaic by the artist William Mitchell. This was sadly destroyed following closure of the venue in 2001. [Heineken UK]

David Noble's sculpture of three seated figures (1963), at the rear of The Towers. [DP275693, James O. Davies]

adjacent three-storey car park block, added in *c.* 1964–5. The main building was repurposed following the completion of a new police station in central Stevenage in 1974. The site and that of the garages are due to be redeveloped.

20 Southgate House (now Vista Tower)

This 15-storey office block, begun in 1963, was the tallest building in Stevenage at the time of its completion in September 1964. It was designed for SDC by Leonard Vincent as a freelance architect, part of the firm Vincent & Gorbing. The Long Ship pub was opened on the lower floors in 1966. The building was altered and converted for residential use in 2015–16.

21 Fire and ambulance station

The fire and ambulance station was built in 1961–2 to designs by the architects of Hertfordshire County Council. It included engine houses, an ambulance park and a hose drying tower.

22 Manulife House

This office block was built for SDC in 1972–3 to designs by Gollins, Melvin, Ward & Partners. Known locally as the 'White Cube', it took its name from its main occupant – the Manulife Life Insurance company. The building was heavily reworked as a Holiday Inn hotel, opened in 2009.

23 St George's Church (now St Andrew and St George)

This church, of striking modern form, was designed for the diocese of St Albans by John Seely (1899–1963) of Seely & Paget. It was begun in July 1956 and formally consecrated on 27 November 1960. The church was rededicated in 1984 and was listed grade II in 1998.

24 Multistorey car park

This building was constructed in 1971–3 to designs by Leonard Vincent and Leslie Aked's team at SDC, and met the increased need for car parking in the town centre. It was built on the site of the Market Square surface car park. The ground floor includes an indoor market, opened in December 1973.

25 Bowes Lyon House youth centre

The youth centre was designed by Leonard Vincent of Vincent & Gorbing and named after Sir David Bowes-Lyon, former Chairman of the Stevenage Youth Trust. The building was begun in March 1964 and opened in April 1965, featuring facilities including a roller rink, coffee bar and sports hall. A skatepark was added on the building's east side in 1978, one of the earliest to be built in Britain. The youth centre survives well, but is programmed for redevelopment in the future.

26 Swimming pool

The swimming pool was designed by Leonard Vincent and his team at SDC and built in 1961–2. It featured a main 110ft- (33.5m) long pool and a training pool, with windows opening onto a terrace. The building was remodelled in 2000–1, and is programmed for future redevelopment.

27 Town Centre Gardens

This large park (also known as Town Gardens) was designed as a facility for the town centre and also as a 'buffer' between the shopping precinct and the housing to its east. It was begun in late summer 1958 and completed in summer 1961. In design, the park made careful use of existing natural features.

28 Arts and leisure centre

This was an innovative scheme, bringing together arts and sports interests in Stevenage. Designed by Raymond Gorbing of Vincent & Gorbing, the centre was begun in June 1974 and completed in late 1975. The building featured areas including a sports hall, bowls hall and 507-seat theatre. It was altered in the early 1990s.

29 Magistrates' court

This low magistrates' court to the rear of Daneshill House was constructed in 1972–3 to designs by the architects of Hertfordshire County Council.

30 Railway station

A dedicated railway station for Stevenage new town, replacing that in the old town to the north, was begun in 1971 and completed in July 1973. It was designed by the Chief Engineer and architects of British Railways Eastern Region, in liaison with SDC. The building was linked to the town centre by an elevated walkway, which passed through the upper level of the arts and leisure centre.

31 Westgate Centre

This 200,000 sq. ft (18,580m²) shopping complex with parking on its upper levels was opened in April 1988 and designed by the firm Renton Howard Wood Levin. The centre was built on the site of the former Westgate surface car park, opened in October 1958.

32 Tesco complex

The Tesco complex was designed by Vincent, Gorbing & Partners and constructed in 1987–8. It included, as well as a Tesco supermarket, smaller shop units, a petrol station and public toilets.

33 Forum Centre

The Forum Centre is a multipurpose scheme built in 1996–7 to designs by Jeff Downes of the Warwick-based firm Corstophine & Wright Kenzie Lovell Ltd. It occupies part of the site once intended for Stevenage's town hall and municipal complex.

Notes

1 Cole with Harwood 2021.

2 Stevenage Development Corporation 1954, 27.

3 SDC, *Purpose: Town Centre Number*, no. 15 (spring 1959), 9; SDC, *Purpose*, no. 8 (summer 1957), 3; Hampson 1959a, 13.

4 Anon. 1956, 83.

5 Burns 1959, 74.

6 Greenwood 1973, 355.

7 Ashby, Margaret ed. 2016, *A Guide to the Forster Country* (Stevenage: The Friends of the Forster Country), 4.

8 Stephenson 1992, 89.

9 Balchin 1980, 69.

10 The National Archives, HLG 91/474 (report of the Stevenage public inquiry, 19 October 1949).

11 Holliday, Clifford, Master Plan 1949, Technical Report, quoted in Balchin 1980, 201.

12 Buchanan, C. D. 1956 'The Road Traffic Problem in Britain', *Town Planning Review*, 26 (no. 4), January, 216.

13 Ibid., 223.

14 Ibid., 221.

15 Burns 1959, 5.

16 Tripp, H. Alker 1942 *Town Planning and Road Traffic* (London: Edward Arnold and Co.), 26.

17 Larsen 2016, 248.

18 Van Der Broek and Bakema 1956, 21–6.

19 Kidder Smith 1957, 173–84.

20 Ministry of Transport 1946, *Design and Layout of Roads in Built-Up Areas* (London: Her Majesty's Stationery Office, 1953 reprint), 32.

21 www.talkingnewtowns.org.uk/content/topics/developing-a-new-town/leonard-vincent-about-stevenage-pedestrianised-town-centre (acc. 29 January 2020).

22 Larsen 2016, 249.

23 TNA, HLG 115/34 (report on the work of SDC, 15 July–15 September 1950).

24 Ibid. (Minutes of meeting, 20 September 1950).

25 Stephenson 1992, 97–8.

26 TNA, HLG 115/34 (minutes of meeting, 20 September 1950).

27 SDC, *Quarterly Bulletin*, no. 1 (1 April 1951), 3–4.

28 TNA, HLG 115/34 (report on the work of SDC, 15 July–15 September 1950).

29 https://www.talkingnewtowns.org.uk/content/topics/developing-a-new-town/mr-ray-gorbing-architect-arguments-pedestrian-town-centre-text (acc. 16 April 2020).

30 TNA, HLG 115/34 (minutes of meeting of 4 April 1951).

31 Balchin 1980, 271.

32 *Architects' Journal*, 133 (issue 3446), 4 May 1961, 634.

33 SDC, *Quarterly Bulletin*, no. 14 (1 July 1954), 2.

34 SDC, *Quarterly Bulletin*, no. 13 (1 April 1954), 2.

35 SDC, *Quarterly Bulletin*, no. 14 (1 July 1954), 2.

36 Vincent 1960, 104; Anon. 1958c, 553.

37 Anon. 1956, 83.

38 Hertfordshire Archives and Local Studies, CNT/ST/5/1/AP/ M47, vol. 1 (memo., 28 November 1968).

39 SDC, *10th Annual Report* (1957) in Burton and Hartly 2003.

40 Patterson 1959b, 25.

41 SDC, *Purpose*, no. 19 (summer 1960), 6.

42 SDC, *Purpose*, no. 13 (autumn 1958), 16.

43 Belsky 1992.

44 For example, see: de Wolfe, Ivor (H. de C. Hastings) 1949 'Townscape, A Plea for an English Visual Philosophy Founded on the True Rock of Sir Uvedale Price', *Architectural Review*, 106 (no. 636), 354–62; Cullen, Gordon 1961 *The Concise Townscape* (London: Architectural Press).

45 Vincent 1959a, 13.

46 https://www.pooleimages.co.uk/carters-tiles (acc. 4 December 2020).

47 Anon. 1959 *Co-operative Architecture 1945–1959* (Manchester: Co-operative Wholesale Society), frontispiece.

48 SDC, *Purpose*, no. 14 (winter 1959 [i.e. 1958–9]), 11; Balchin 1980, 277.

49 Hampson 1959a, 16.

50 Anon. 1958c, 553.

51 Bilbow 1959, 365; Bilbow, Thomas 1959 'London Transport Garage at Hatfield', *Official Architecture and Planning*, 22 (no. 4), April, 182.

52 Vincent 1959a, 11; Vincent 1960, 103.

53 Vincent 1959a, 11.

54 *Stevenage Pictorial*, 16 October 1959, 22.

55 Anon. 1958b, 7.

56 Stallabrass 1959, 22.

57 Childs, D. Rigby and Boyne, D. A. C. A. 1952 'Bristol', *Architects' Journal*, 116 (no. 3005), 2 October, 397–9.

58 McCallum, Ian ed. 1957 'Machine-Made America', *Architectural Review*, 121 (no. 724), May, 295–93; Brawne, Michael and Craig, Alan 1957 'Walls off the Peg', *Architectural Review*, 122 (no. 728), September, 166–87.

59 SDC, *Purpose: Town Centre Number*, no. 15 (spring 1959), 3.

60 Vincent 1959a, 13.

61 Browne 1957, 123. See also SDC, *Purpose*, no. 9 (autumn 1957), 11.

62 Vincent 1959a, 12.

63 https://www.britishpathe.com/video/new-town/query/ stevenage (acc. 15 April 2020).

64 Hampson 1959a, 15; Patterson 1959b, 25.

65 Vincent 1959a, 13.

66 Stallabrass 1959, 22.

67 Ibid., 23.

68 Ibid., 24.

69 HALS, CNT/ST/1/2/41 (report of 8 March 1955); draft text, Harwood, Elain *New Towns* (Historic England/Liverpool University Press), forthcoming.

70 Stallabrass 1959, 24.

71 Ibid., 22.

72 TNA, HLG 115/140 (document of 6 March 1961).

73 *Stevenage Pictorial*, 1 December 1961, 20. See also *Stevenage Gazette*, 30 August 1963, 1.

74 *Stevenage Pictorial*, 13 July 1962, 3.

75 *Stevenage Gazette*, 1 January 1965, 3; SDC, *19th Annual Report* (1966), in Burton and Hartly 2003.

76 Anon. 1958d, 862.

77 HALS, CNT/ST/5/1/AP/T29, vol. 2 (letter, 17 October 1960).

78 SDC, *Purpose*, no. 21 (winter 1961 [i.e. 1960/1]), 10.

79 HALS, CNT/ST/5/1/AP/T41, vol. 1 (notes of meeting, 18 September 1962).

80 *Stevenage Pictorial*, 6 October 1961, 9.

81 *Stevenage Pictorial*, 6 October 1961, 8; *Stevenage Gazette*, 29 September 1961, 13.

82 *Stevenage Pictorial*, 12 October 1962, 1.

83 SDC, *Purpose*, no. 26 (autumn 1962), 11.

84 *Architects' Journal*, 137 (issue 7), 13 February 1963, 363.

85 *Stevenage Pictorial*, 11 May 1962, 3.

86 Ibid.

87 *Stevenage Gazette*, 5 June 1964, 1.

88 Anon. 1966, 345.

89 Ibid., 346.

90 Ackroyd 1969, 657.

91 HALS, CNT/ST/5/1/AP/T29, vol. 1 (note of meeting, 7 September 1960).

92 SDC, *Purpose*, no. 24 (March 1962), 5.

93 HALS, CNT/ST/5/1/AP/B62, vol. 1 (notes of meeting, 4 January 1973).

94 Pers. comm. (David Rixson, formerly of Vincent & Gorbing).

95 Balchin 1980, 283.

96 Vincent 1959a, 12; Vincent 1960, 105.

97 SDC, *Quarterly Bulletin*, no. 10 (1 July 1953), 12.

98 Adie 1976, 1083.

99 Mullan 1980, 31.

100 Stevenage Borough Council 1981 *Stevenage District Plan: Shopping Topic Report* (Stevenage: Stevenage Borough Council), section 5.2 [copy in British Library].

101 SBC planning records (2/0256/84).

102 http://www.stevenage.gov.uk/ content/15953/26685/26727/27889 (acc. 30 January 2020).

103 Hampson 1959a, 13.

104 *Stevenage Pictorial*, 1 January 1960, 1.

105 HALS, CNT/ST/5/AP/P15, vol. 3 (press notice, December 1964).

106 Quoted in Balchin 1980, 278.

107 Ibid.

108 SDC, *Purpose*, no. 13 (autumn 1958), 3.

109 Ibid.

110 Ibid.

111 *Stevenage Pictorial*, 8 May 1959, 18.

112 *Stevenage Pictorial*, 20 May 1960, 1.

113 *Architects' Journal*, 133 (issue 3441), 30 March 1961, 452; *Stevenage Gazette*, 4 October 1963, 1.

114 *Stevenage Pictorial*, 8 April 1960, 15; SDC, *Purpose*, no. 18 (spring 1960), 3.

115 SDC, *Purpose*, no. 27 (winter 1963 [i.e. 1962/3]), 12; SDC, *Purpose*, no. 31 (summer 1964), 7; SDC, *15th Annual Report* (1962), in Burton and Hartly 2003.

116 Balchin 1980, 345.

117 SDC, *15th Annual Report* (1962), in Burton and Hartly 2003.

118 Burns 1959, pl. 80.

119 See, for instance, a film commissioned by SDC in 1971: http:// www.eafa.org.uk/catalogue/2431 (acc. 3 March 2021).

120 Anon. 1960, 127.

121 Hardy 1959, 18.

122 Anon. 1956, 83; Anon. 1958c, 553.

123 Vincent 1959a, 11.

124 Stephenson, Gordon 1985 'Architecture, Town Planning and Civic Design', *Town Planning Review*, 56 (no. 2), April, 156.

125 *Newcastle Journal*, 22 February 1968, 6.

126 Robinson 1962, 53.

127 Balchin 1980, 289.

128 Browne 1957, 126.

129 Balchin 1980, 279.

130 HALS, CNT/ST/5/1/AP/M47, vol. 1 (memo., 28 November 1968).

131 Ibid.

132 TNA, HLG 115/34 (memo., 14 March 1951).

133 Burns 1959, 72–3.

134 *Stevenage Pictorial*, 6 March 1959, 22.

135 SDC, *Purpose*, no. 13 (autumn 1958), 12.

136 Robinson 1962, 51 and 53.

137 Ibid., 52.

138 *The Surveyor*, 24 September 1971, 32–4.

139 Pers. comm. (David Rixson, formerly of Vincent & Gorbing).

140 Hampson 1959b, 29.

141 '"Joyride" Expresses New Town's Youth', *The Times*, 30 September 1958, 6; Hampson 1959b, 29.

142 Lock and Ellis 2020, 63.

143 SBC 2019 *Future Town, Future Transport: A Transport Strategy for Stevenage* (Stevenage: Stevenage Borough Council).

144 Stevenage Better (Stevenage Development Board) (2021) https://stevenage-even-better.com/tag/development-in-stevenage/ (acc. 1 March 2021).

145 Ibid.

146 Pers. comm. (SBC).

Select bibliography and further reading

Ackroyd, Peter 1969 'Youth Centres at Withywood and Stevenage', *Architects' Journal*, 150 (issue 37), 10 September, 645–60

Adie, Donald 1976 'Building Study: Three Sports Centres', *Architects' Journal*, 164 (issue 49), 8 December, 1075–88

Anon. 1956 'Proposed Town Centre, Stevenage', *Architects' Journal*, 124 (issue 3203), 19 July, 83–4

Anon. 1957 'Stevenage New Town Centre', *Architectural Review*, 121 (issue 720), 1 January, liii

Anon. 1958a 'Planning Schemes: Town Centre, Stevenage', *Architectural Review*, 123 (issue 732), 1 January, 13–15

Anon. 1958b '"Planner's Dream" at New Towns', *The Times*, 23 May, 7

Anon. 1958c 'First Shops Opening in Stevenage Town Centre', *The Surveyor and Municipal and County Engineer,* 117 (no. 3449), 31 May, 553–4

Anon. 1958d 'Britain's First Pedestrian Centre', *Architects' Journal*, 127 (issue 3301), 5 June, 862

Anon. 1958e 'Stevenage New Town Centre', *Town and Country Planning*, 26 (issue 8), 1 August, 308

Anon. 1959 [*attrib.* Vincent, L. G.], 'Stevenage Town Centre', *The Contract Journal*, 23 April, 384–5

Anon. 1960 'Stevenage Town Centre', *The Builder*, 198 (no. 6087), 15 January, 126–8

Anon. 1961a I 'Office block, Stevenage', *Architect & Building News*, 31 May, 713–5

Anon. 1961b II 'Post office, Stevenage', *Architect & Building News*, 31 May, 721–4

Anon. 1962 'Stevenage Out-Patient Centre', *The Hospital*, 58 (no. 3), March, 147–151

Anon. 1963 'Bowling Centre at Stevenage', *Architects' Journal*, 137 (issue 10), 6 March, 521–7

Anon. 1964 'Swimming Baths at Stevenage', *Architects' Journal*, 140 (issue 20), 11 November, 1143–51

Anon. 1966 'Youth Centre at Stevenage', *Architects' Journal*, 143 (issue 5), 2 February, 341–56

Anon. 1973 'Stevenage Station', *The Architect*, 3 (no. 11), November, 52

Balchin, Jack 1980 *First New Town: An Autobiography of the Stevenage Development Corporation 1946–1980* (Stevenage: Stevenage Development Corporation)

Belsky, Franta 1992 *Sculpture* (London: Zwemmer), n.p.

Bilbow, Thomas 1959 'London Transport Garage for Stevenage', *Official Architecture and Planning*, 22 (no. 8), August, 365

Bilsborough, Joe 1980 'The History of the First New Town', *Building Trades Journal*, June, 15–16

Browne, Kenneth 1957 'Space to Let: Plan for Advertising in a New Town', *Architectural Review*, 122 (no. 727), August, 122–6

Burns, Wilfred 1959 *British Shopping Centres: New Trends in Layout and Distribution* (London: Leonard Hill Ltd)

Burton, Anthony and Hartly, Joyce eds 2003 *The New Towns Record 1946–2002* (London: IDOX Information Services) (CD/DVD compilation, RIBA)

Calladine, Anthony 1999 *Stevenage New Town Centre: The Conservation of Modern Buildings* (unpublished MA thesis in Architectural Conservation, De Montfort University, 1999) [copy in Historic England Archive]

Cole, Emily, with Harwood, Elain 2021 *The New Town Centre, Stevenage, Hertfordshire: Architecture and Significance* (Historic England Research Report, no. 267-2020) [available online via: https://historicengland.org.uk/research/research-results/research-reports/]

Greenwood, Lord 1973, 'New Towns' [lecture delivered 24 January 1973], *Journal of the Royal Society of Arts*, 121 (no. 5202), 355

Hampson, T. 1959a 'The Stevenage Town Centre', *Town and Country Planning*, January, 13–16

Hampson, T. 1959b 'The Heart of a Town', in SDC, *Purpose: Town Centre Number*, 15, spring, 27–9

Hardy, G. E. 1959 'An Engineer's Problems', in SDC, *Purpose: Town Centre Number*, 15, spring, 14–18

Harwood, E. 2015 *Space, Hope and Brutalism, English Architecture 1945–1975* (London: Yale University Press)

Kidder Smith, G. E. 1957 'Vällingby', *Architectural Record*, 121 (no. 4), April, 173–84

Larsen, Kristin E. 2016 *Community Architect: The Life and Vision of Clarence S. Stein* (Ithaca and London: Cornell University Press)

Lock, Katy and Ellis, Hugh 2020 *New Towns: The Rise, Fall and Rebirth* (London: RIBA)

Marshall, Nigel 1972 'Stevenage Town Centre and Town Garden', *Landscape Design*, 100, November, 33–5

Morrison, Kathryn A. 2003 *English Shops and Shopping* (New Haven and London: Yale University Press)

Morrison, Kathryn A. and Minnis, John 2012 *Carscapes: The Motor Car, Architecture and Landscape in England* (New Haven and London: Yale University Press)

Mullan, Bob 1980 *Stevenage Ltd: Aspects of the Planning and Politics of Stevenage New Town, 1945–78* (London, Boston and Henley: Routledge & Kegan Paul)

Osborn, F. and Whittick, A. 1977 *New Towns: Their Origins, Achievements and Progress* (London: L. Hill)

Patterson, Gordon 1959a 'Work in Progress: Stevenage Town Centre', *Journal of the Institute of Landscape Architects*, 1 February, 10

Patterson, Gordon 1959b 'Town Centre Landscape', in SDC, *Purpose: Town Centre Number*, 15, spring, 25–6

Robinson, Kenneth J. 1962 'The Town of Tomorrow: It's Here Today', *Sunday Times*, 11 November, 51–3

Rowe, Alan H. 1973 'Stevenage – A New Concept', *Built Environment*, 2 (no. 8), August, 464–6

Stallabrass, V. 1959 'The Shopping Centre', in SDC, *Purpose: Town Centre Number*, 15, spring, 22–4

Stephenson, Gordon 1992 *in* Christina DeMarco (ed.), *On a Human Scale: A Life in City Design* (South Fremantle: Fremantle Arts Centre Press)

Stevenage Development Corporation 1954 *Building the New Town of Stevenage* (Stevenage: Stevenage Development Corporation)

Van Der Broek, J. H. and Bakema, J. B.1956 'The Lijnbaan at Rotterdam', *Town Planning Review*, April, 21–6

Vincent, L. G. 1959a 'Planning and Design' in SDC, *Purpose: Town Centre Number*, 15, spring, 11–13

Vincent, L. G. 1959b 'Town Centre', *Architecture and Building*, 34 (no. 6), 206–13

Vincent, L. G. 1959c 'The Town Centre, Stevenage', *Architectural Design*, 29 (issue 7), 1 July, 259

Vincent, Leonard G. 1960 'The Town Centre, Stevenage', *Town Planning Review*, 31 (no. 2), July, 103–8

Ward, Stephen V. 2016 'Stevenage' in *The Peaceful Path: Building Garden Cities and New Towns* (Hatfield: University of Hertfordshire Press), 182–238

Informed Conservation Series

This popular Historic England series highlights the special character of some of our most important historic areas and the development of the pressures they are facing. There are over 30 titles in the series, some of which look at whole towns such as Bridport, Coventry and Margate or distinctive urban districts, such as the Jewellery Quarter in Birmingham and Ancoats in Manchester, while others focus on particular building types in a particular place. A few are national in scope focusing, for example, on English school buildings and garden cities.

The purpose of the series is to raise awareness of the interest and importance of aspects of the built heritage of towns and cities undergoing rapid change or large-scale regeneration. A particular feature of each book is a final chapter that focuses on conservation issues, identifying good examples of the re-use of historic buildings and highlighting those assets or areas for which significant challenges remain.

As accessible distillations of more in-depth research, they also provide a useful resource for heritage professionals tackling, as many of the books do, places and building types that have not previously been subjected to investigation from the historic environment perspective. As well as providing a lively and informed discussion of each subject, the books also act as advocacy documents for Historic England and its partners in protecting historic places and keeping them alive for current and future generations.

More information on each of the books in the series and on forthcoming titles can be found on the Historic England website.

HistoricEngland.org.uk